Tango Waves

Omega and Alpha dance in the dark to the song of evolutionary political economy

Hardy Hanappi

Tango Waves

ISBN: 9798335452953

DEDICATION

This book is dedicated to my family

Tango Waves

CONTENTS

Tango Waves

PREFACE

Please read this book, it is worth the effort. Because in many ways this book is rather peculiar, it is a strange brew. It combines a storyline of an emerging love affair with the evolution of the political dynamics of our contemporary society. In doing so, it mixes belletristic elements with scientifically inspired analysis and philosophical excurses. The twenty chapters are meant to be little waves that together form a longer wave. Politically this longer wave follows the long downturn of progressive politics that started in 1980, only the last chapter is meant to give some hope. On the individual level love turns out to be a lasting - evolutionary changing
- force throughout the whole wave.

The characters in this book are all fictional, they only live between the pages of this book. Thus, they are real. I have tried to follow their thoughts, to creep into their minds. Not too deep, of course, since this is meant to be a short and readable book. Each chapter shall be an intellectual meal: Read it and take some time to digest it, usually it is dense stuff. Contrary to the scientific papers that I am used to write I do not use footnotes in this book. This is owed to the task of staying belletristic. To compensate for the missing additional information in footnotes I have added some pages after the last chapter, which I called Mysterious Links. There you find some internet links to some music and to some (of my) research papers relevant for the respective chapter. With no comment, since this is only for nerds – like myself.

Knowingly and not-knowing many people in my social environment have contributed to this book – all above my family. I have to thank them all; and I have to excuse for the chaotic style in which it partially appears. It simply is the style in which I write: When I write a page, I do not know what I will write on the next page, not to speak of the name of the next chapter. In other words, I did not have a predetermined plan. The course of the book emerged while it was written. This style probably is my tribute to improvising jazz musicians. I hope there are readers who like such free-wheeling spirit.

Finally, I have to thank my friends at the publishing house that dared to publish a book like this, something that is proud to be in between all established genres. Please read this book, it is worth the effort.

Athens, June 2024 Hardy Hanappi

1 TEXT

The individual had breakfast. It had a name – but this name will not be used. It would always add colour to the individual. And there are no more specific colours in this world. Just a mess of crying contradictions.
After breakfast the individual did not take its guns. It had no gun. Only characters in movies
and US citizens own guns. The guns of stately gunmen, of 'gendarmes', are public guns.

When the individual started to speak, it was immediately clear that English was not its original tongue. It probably spoke to its smartphone – or to one of the other individuals in the background. It did not matter. It never mattered. There were times when the individual talked a lot. It never had learned to listen, not really. The individual had always only imitated: What his mother and father did, how others behaved and communicated. Its early imitations were only influenced by two feelings, pain and lust. A friend in these ages said, 'You are an animal!'.

When the individual looked in a mirror, it did not see itself. It only saw a human face, a friend. But the friend was a mirror too. Unfortunately - or fortunately – there were many friends and enemies, each one producing a somewhat different mirror image. Each image provoking a somewhat different emotional reaction inside the individual. The individual was nothing but a basket full of contradictions, emotional contradictions. Was it more than that at all? Or was it just this unorganized collection of communicative interactions that repeatedly hammered on its perceptions' apparatus. To ask itself such a question, it needed an inner language. As a teenager it had started to develop such an inner language. Unconscious imitations slowed down and made room for a selection of acceptable originals worth to be copied – just another set of unsurmountable contradictions. Looking inside itself was just as chaotic as the communication noise of the culture that surrounded the individual. And noise it was – indeed. But seen from the opposite perspective, the individual was perfectly adapted to its environment: chaotic and purified from any thought beyond pain and lust. It was caught as a particle in its culture, it was a *cultural animal*.

But though each single individual was lost in its culture, acting as an ensemble of stream-lined robots this cultural entity gains power. The chaotic background on which this power is built seduces the individual to think that this power can point in any direction. But in the morning the individual has had its breakfast. It had a breakfast that somehow was produced by a large group of interacting individuals spread all over the world until the resulting products finally were exchanged for the money that the individual spent in diverse shops. There was the food chain and its underlying money chain – both of them essentially global.

The cultural entity is characterized by – and loosely encapsulated in – the limits of acquaintance and communication. During its lifetime the average individual encounters a very limited number of other individuals in a direct physical way. It is the contradiction between this physical constraint and the overwhelming information overflow, the appearance of chaos, which produces the contemporary age of alienation.

Around the globe, on each continent, there are many distinctive cultural entities. Their borderlines are drawn along the sometimes-vague language barriers. Strict borders given by possible physical movements, by geography, are extended by speaking, by understanding, by recognizing similar habits. Another contradiction emerges: The own social identity opposes that of the strangers; the foreign cultural entity to some extent always remains an unknown ambience.

As described above, the individual is lost. It is so intensively lost that it often has completely substituted its consciousness of being an individual by the common ideological mirage. In this case, this ideological mirage - basically a result of the communicative network, which accompanies the economic network of the cultural entity – serves as an interpretation scheme for all incoming new information. While the visibility of the global economic network structure is necessarily restricted by the individuals locally bound existence and perception capabilities anyway, the emerging additional blindness stemming from predefined interpretation schemes pushes cultural tribes typically into states of highly manipulable, volatile limbo.

It is the inner economic structure of these cultural entities - namely their falling apart into ruling, exploiting classes and governed, exploited classes of individuals – which determines the major direction of ideological manipulation of the cultural entity. The ruling class, which nowadays commands an extremely efficient toolset of mass media, shapes dominating world views and interpretation schemes of its whole *tribe.*'.

2 OMEGA

Omega laid back in his armchair and looked at the words of his text in front of him. He had his laptop on his thighs, he looked amused. 'Strong stuff!', he thought, 'perhaps a bit too compressed, too dense.'. He would not change it, he knew it, he always would stick to the first version in which the words poured out of his mind. He was rather vain – at least in this respect. Doubt, some distance to the originality of his product would be in place. But - no, not now. He put the laptop on the desk, stood up and went to the kitchen. He was alone, a lonely individual. Did he always only write stories about himself? What he wanted was quite the opposite: He was obsessed with the wish to grasp the general frameworks, to understand the deeper lying truths. You always walk with contradictions, he thought, not knowing to whom he spoke. In the kitchen he decided to have breakfast, it was six a clock in the morning. He smiled: 'The individual had breakfast.'

While individuality is self-evident for every naïve person, its use as a concept to understand human society is far from innocent. When Daniel Defoe constructed Robinson Crusoe, his narrative corresponded to Rousseau's dream of a lost natural state of peaceful and independent human individuals. As a young boy Omega had loved to read Defoe's book, though he preferred to see himself as Friday, Crusoe's wild native companion. The transition from naïve to native is easy, just take a dot, expand it to a 't' and squeeze it in in front of the remaining 'ï'. His mind tumbled into a different area of mystery: language. But he preferred to stay focussed: individuality. When he was older, he found out that individuality was not just an experience but also a theoretical concept used in the communication sphere. The first encounter was at the age of seventeen. He had some friends who were fascinated by anarchism, read Kropotkin, and had some interesting disputes with a somewhat older friend who called himself a communist. Omega found both attitudes interesting. The main difference had been that the older guy insisted on the existence and dynamics of class structures, while the anarchistic younger ones emphasized the free will of each individual as the ultimate decision criterion in a desirable society. The appeal of the latter attitude partly was owed to Omega's dream at this age to become an artist; artists are only controlled by their innate, superior abilities to produce aesthetic artwork. They are individuals, he thought, they do not allow society to disturb their mission. Three years later Omega found his former insisting on individuality rather embarrassing, he now was reading Karl Marx - and not Kropotkin. Marx explicitly denounced the dreams of Rousseau and his followers in economics as 'Robinsonades', as an inadequate image of how the working of societies can be understood. From that time onwards, Omega was sure that the use of the concept of individuality as a starting point for a theory of political economy was a dead end. As he learned during his study years this dead end had established itself in academia with the name 'microeconomics', he called it microtheology.

Omega's mind suddenly made a jump: A woman emerged like a sudden flash. He did not really know her; he just had met this appearance yesterday at the train station. Now he saw her face again, getting clearer as it approached from the back of his memory, from somewhere deep in his brain. A mix of memory and his mind: I always fix a female individual in my brain with three steps, he confessed to himself. I'm afraid, I cannot do wholistic perception. First, I perceive the silhouette, the shape of the borderline of the female body. At the train station, yesterday, my perception was caught by her silhouette as she left the train some twenty meters in front of me. It was completely convincing: Just this necessary bit away from commonly praised perfection; this is what should have been called 'individual perfection'. My attention immediately goes into second gear. The second element then is the face. The woman and I move in opposite directions, approached each other. And her face really struck me. I had to hold back my excitement, had to force me to stop my blunt staring at her face. I turned my head, pretended to look into a train window to find somebody. She passed by. Now I was free to turn again to watch her moving away from me. This enables the third stage of elementary perception: I could look how she walked. The walk of a woman reveals her deepest dynamic habits. The silliest persiflage of this element of perception is presented at the catwalk of fashion models. It is so disgusting that I would sign any petition aiming to forbid it. But this woman yesterday walked with a combination of strength and elegance, of determination and flexible correction; I was standing there speechless until she vanished in another stream of travelers. At this moment it was unnecessary to think about possibilities to see her again. I had met her, and that was good enough. Now, today, when her face suddenly jumped right into his internal perception, the wish to meet her again was immediately there, was strong.

For a whole week Omega went to the train station every day at the same hour when he had first seen her – in vain. Then it became a habit. Whenever he could, he escaped to the platforms of the train station, strolling around without a specific goal. He appreciated this contrast to most other people who were so busy to be somewhere in time. His only companions were a few homeless occupying some dry corners of the train station, but even these shy and pointless creatures were sometimes stressed by the sight of policemen.

At home, Omega continued to write his text. His attention had moved on, individuality did not interest him too much anymore. Cultural entities, how they are constituted, and their physical and communicative visibility, all became his new topic. In particular, their volatility, and their instrumentalization by religious and fascist leaders, seemed to be an urgent issue. Intellectual excitement is a drug, he knew. What were smartphones doing to societies in this respect? Modern information technologies were a blessing and a curse – he was back at his old specialty: contradictions. To disentangle all the knots was not an option. What Omega could do was to walk around this ball of complicated, interwoven threads, look at it from all sides and – yes – write an inextricable text. Somewhere far behind the text was lingering a treasure: Was it the face of a woman?

3 ALPHA

She was a working girl, north of England way. This was what Alpha thought of herself when she was fifteen years old. And she was. She still loved the Beatles, in particular George. For her, he never will die. So far, Alpha had travelled her life in a rather straightway. As every day she now sat in the bus taking her to the office of the insurance firm where she worked. It was
7.30. She was a bit bored. Too many people, too much gossip all around, useless noises coming from useless people, every individual occupied by its own, narrow ego trip. But at the same time, everybody was boasting around stupid and noisy arguments as if somebody really had a say. It was not really anger that she felt, but rather a sad boredness. Alpha always had goals. Not just higher salary, better apartment, eventually a nicer guy. No, she wanted more – a bit like the girl in the Beatles song. She knew it was somehow a dream, somehow illusionary, but she wanted to hit it big. The opportunity would come – and she would grasp it. Her parents had given her the name Alpha, they expected her to reach some kind of top. Her time would come, and on her slow ascending path she always stayed alert, looking around if her moment comes into sight. Alpha was quick, pretty quick – and rather pretty too. At least this was how she always had perceived herself.
This had been fifteen years ago. Now she was in her early thirties. Was she still pretty? Was
she still a 'girl'? Probably not. Did men still turn their heads when she walked by? Last week

at the train station she had shortly noticed such an incident. The bus drivers were on strike, so she had to take the train – somewhat earlier than her usual bus. Leaving the train, stepping on the platform, turning … and suddenly she saw this

man staring at her. He came closer and closer. He gave her the impression of being hypnotized; or was he just fascinated by her? It had been a long time since she had cultivated her feeling of being magic. But now she liked it, damned, she had missed it. And he was a good-looking fellow. If she was a nine, then he was an eight. Good enough for a young woman in her thirties that had lost the attribute 'girl'. A closer look at his face now showed her his age: five to ten years older than she, she estimated. Adequate. She wondered with which sentence he would approach her, would open the first chat. Then suddenly, at a distance of only a few meters, he turned his face to the side of the train window. He pretended to look at someone still in the train, tried to find a known face. But she immediately knew this was a fake. There was nobody left in the train, he only wanted to avoid coming into direct contact with her. Why? She walked a bit faster now, passed him by at a safe distance and with a firm look at the platform exit. Idiot! Forget him. Or was there something wrong with her – at shorter distance? No, never start to doubt. It only kills your energy.
She had had this experience a few times only in her life: A sudden wave of doubt, of despair about something she had done or something that she was in the eyes of others. A moment where she had the undeniable need to reinvent herself to jump out of this hole of depression. A new kind of energy had quickly to be mobilized for a new kind of Alpha. The standstill of the old kind of energy had to be as short as possible, only as long as the moment in Tango dancing when both dancers are frozen like marble statues before they continue in a different direction. All elements of the freeze then had instantaneously to be forgotten. It struck her that she now suddenly remembered this man. He was already purged from her brain, she had thought.

Her current lover was not bad, anyway. He had been the result of the escape from such a typical breakdown blizzard in her relationship network. Over the years the exchanges, the empty conversations and more and more backward oriented topics with her childhood friends became more and more paralyzing. She had tried to avoid contacts, to stay at home, to read books instead. But she not only became lonely, she felt lonely. Then Frank entered her life. He was a younger nephew of her father, son of an aunt, which she barely knew because her family lived in Cornwall and they never visited them. There was a profound bad mood between her father and his sister since he had inherited the house of their parents in London, while she had to be content with a lesser sum of money. Her father used to point out to her that the cost to maintain the house were so high that actually she was better off. On the few occasions when the two families met neither Frank nor Alpha felt to be obliged to take sides in this dispute. Then Frank moved to London because he was offered an attractive job in a real estate company. Suddenly he had money and he was easy going. He invited Alpha first for a coffee, later to go out at night. He was a somewhat lazy guy, too lazy for the burden to make a new girl. He made the easy choice: Check out if your cousin is a good company. And they were lucky enough to meet at the time when her old friendship network was in a dead-end street. Soon, a few weekends later, she found out that his sexual capabilities surmounted her expectations. He also seemed to be very content to team up with her. He rapidly had collected a group of colleagues hanging around in real estate businesses (or even more criminally inclined waters), which substituted her old friends. Apart from sex, Frank did not need her much. He really was easy going, always good for some light entertainment, generous and laughing loud when he liked a joke. She also enjoyed the looseness of their entanglement, some shallow flirts with Frank's friends, talking gossip with their wives. At her job in the insurance firm, she worked more seriously on her career. She became team leader of a group, was invited to important board meetings, and the like. It was a world clearly distinguished from Frank's world – he took the car in the morning, she took the bus – maintaining the distance in time, space and personalities of the two. But, to be honest, Alpha already felt that the distance in her relationships was already transforming from 'great freedom' to 'great ennui'.

Frank loved sports, though his legs were too thin for soccer and his arms were too thin for tennis. What he liked most was to watch a tight endgame. Curiously enough, in real life he never recognized when a game entered the stage of an endgame. This was a disadvantage in the games played by real estate managers, it probably was the reason why he never advanced in his job. He remained waiting for the start of the endgame until time was over. Finally, he retired at the same position in the company at which he started. Well, just another way to endure a pre-determined endgame. With respect to Alpha, he would accept the endgame as he later did accept that his career ladder lay flat on the ground. But in the moment, he was not knowing that endgames exist in real life too.

4 LOVE

Love has too many faces to be taken serious as a concept. Even at the level of a specific feeling of a particular individual it cannot be nailed down to something that can be identified across space and time – not to speak about across individuals. And love at the level of the species? This is communism, or the humanistic side of Catholicism. As soon as it is uttered as a wish – All you need is love – it has to be constrained by rule books that state how generalized love has to be organized; be it the rules of socialist governance, be it the ten commandments. The fluid idea of love escapes all organisation in an extremely radical way. Of course, love has catalysts: Sexual desires, birth of a child, and more mundane sources of lust. In this unspecified way love can be understood as the name for the motor behind all the activities of individuals of a species. It moves us towards progress, or in the case of feudal religion, of Catholicism, towards *God*. The difference lies in the implied constraining rule system.

The blatant contradiction between the name of the goal and the set of organisational constraints that it necessarily entails is a surprise. It makes life difficult. Love is an exercise in jumping into unknown waters, in all varieties and on all levels.

A promising strategy to approach a non-concept is to look for its opposite, its mirror image. The opposite of silence could be noise, which adds the dimension of multiple sounds to the trivial opposition loudness. The opposition to love could be hate or indifference. At the level of the individual *indifference* is more opposed than hate, since it not only reverses the direction of a relationship, but even cancels the existence of any relationship. Thus, any dispute on the nature of a relationship is immediately cancelled too. If love goes bust on the individual level it often goes through these two stages: from hate to indifference.

Ignoring religions, ideologic relicts of feudalism, generalised love as communism has as opposition what Hobbes called the 'bellum omnium contra omnes', war between each single individual against each other individual. In this mirror image the role of all catalysts of love disappears. What the human species has inherited from the animal kingdom – sex, child care, cooperation, liking things, etc. – is deleted. The Leviathan that Hobbes was describing, he ascribed to a 'natural' state of affairs of human individuals. Thus, he turned the argument around to denounce human individuals as being unable to organise their love, as incapable to survive without a feudal monarch, a ruling class that governs them. 372 years after Hobbes, it is clear that he did not describe the set of human individuals with their inborn fatal deficiencies, but rather had a vision of the set of capitalist firms, which in his time were just emerging in merchant capitalism.

The excuse that capitalist propaganda typically uses to justify the historical necessity of 'bellum omnium contra omnes' is that these battles between firms enforce innovation. Firm owners are forced to introduce new labour time saving production techniques and have to come up with new types of products. And indeed, as a look back reveals, this justification has been correct for a very long time. But there have been side effects that now seem to override the traditional benefits of the historical mission of capitalism. On the global level the 'catalysts of love', the incentives for a beneficial global governance organisation, seem to have completely vanished; the disorganising force of nation state driven wars are taking over. The world wars of the 20th century now appear as just a prelude to the next dark age. The love is gone! When in the seventies of that century Ian Dury sang that he lived on 'sex, drugs and rock-n-roll', this was the outcry of an individual that longed for catalysts for love and lust. The promises of the sixties were already fading away, Punk took over. The further cultural collapse then became a part of the worldwide political shift to the right. The relationship between capitalist firms is the opposite of love and as firm encompassing political entities nationalist states fight against each other - first as economic competitors but soon also in wars.

A finer grained structure of love occurs within a nationalist state. On the one hand, the exploited class is the natural enemy of its domestic exploiters, thus 'no love'. On the other hand, as citizens of the same nationalist state the exploited class can be an ally in the fight against other nationalist states, thus a strange sympathy between opposing classes stipulated by government – commonly called nationalism – might emerge. On both sides of the local barricades this opportunistic sympathy causes confusion. In particular the glue between the individual particles of the exploited class, its loving unity, is getting cracks. On the side of the exploiting class these cracks more often occur between age groups: younger members not yet leading the continuous exploitation battle at the factory floor might feel sympathy for youngsters from the exploited class and young people in foreign nation states. Love is in the air. Therefore, love within classes, within groups, is week love. It is experienced as such also because individuals compare it with the strong bonds that love at the individual level is expected to build. Today the human world is developing into a network of firm-like egos, of enemies, and each enemy at the bottom of its soul is longing for love.

5 THE TRIP

Omega stared at the screen in front of him. All that is trivial, he murmured. Why do I write texts like this one? Do I personally need love? Whose love? Do I want to belong to somebody, to a woman, to a group? 'Probably yes', he whispered. It cannot be trivial, there is too much sentiment, too much of my own life, of my blood in these lines. I desperately want to understand love, understand myself – and I dramatically fail to do so. If a lost individual states that it is lost, this leads nowhere. At best this sells as a postmodern drama, as a culmination of unsatisfying uselessness. He giggled; he hated postmodernism.

Omega turned away, turned away from the laptop, suddenly knew that he needed fresh air. It was Sunday, why not go for a walk? Or, even better, drive somewhere in the countryside, sit on a bench in a country inn. Feeling lonely there. He could ask his friend Llewellyn if he wanted to join. Good idea, he thought and texted Llewellyn. His friend had always plans on a Sunday, but was always ready to change his plans. Omega would fetch him with his car and they would make a trip.

Llewellyn was a friend since his school days. When they were fifteen Omega gave him the name 'Llewellyn' because he found that his real name, Anthony Miller, was completely inadequate for a personality like him. Omega liked naming, he did it with all persons close enough to him to play a role in his life. The double 'L' at the beginning of a name fascinated him, so 'Llewellyn' carried the message that this friend was his best friend. Boys always need a best friend, he was convinced. Llewellyn was rather shy and most of the time Omega was introverted too, spoke little. So, the couple became known as a decent pair of interesting, but quiet guys. Only their peculiar names usually raised a smile. In rare situations

Omega surprised his company with a breakout. Then all the ideas and feelings that he had silently collected over weeks in the back of his brain were pouring out of his mouth, an unstoppable monologue was drowning his friends. In these moments only Llewellyn was able to follow Omega's thoughts and associations – he knew his friend. The others just were petrified by Omega's unexpected presence. Shortly after Omega had dubbed Anthony Miller as 'Llewellyn', it was Llewellyn who invented the name 'Omega' for the boy formerly practically unknown. Llewellyn liked to discover structures, to formalise observations, he had a foible for mathematics. His best friend, his unexpected breakouts, gave him a thrill and Omega was the name of electric resistance. Moreover, it was the last letter in the Greek alphabet, being the end, the limit of alphabetic order. His admiration for his best friend could not have been better packed up than in this ambivalence of being the last in biological order – in that way Omega was used for Omega-animals in biology - and at the same time being the ultimate expression for the finiteness of the world, which was one of his most beloved convictions. So, in short, Omega became Omega not only in Llewellyn's view, but also in Omega's self-perception. Everybody else followed.

All these memories! Omega locked the door of his apartment and took the elevator to the garage. He should have walked, he knew, he was getting a little fat and lazy. He was content with his car, it worked. His previous car had been a cause of periodic trouble. The traffic on the way to Llewellyn's house – he had inherited a nice little house in the suburb from his parents – was horrific. He called Llewellyn again to tell him he would be a little late. While driving, actually more stopping than driving, his brain invisibly still worked on the text he had written at home. Yes, the other cars were something like firm-like egos, trying to be nasty wherever they could. Sometimes a driver was polite and let him smuggle in in front of him in a queue; but he was sure that this was only a dirty trick with a hidden agenda. Was he already like them? In fact, cross down traffic was a perfect mirror image of the modern confusion in the world. All the cars got stuck, the rulers of the world took their private jets to fly from holiday destinations to their board rooms and back. But at least there was this old Jimi Hendrix song 'Cross down traffic' that eased his soul. He turned the music louder.

Llewellyn was already waiting on the pavement in front of his house. He looked elated. After Llewellin had entered the car Omega felt somehow more at ease. The dangling conversation that enrolled freed him from the spell of second thoughts on the text, his 'good-morning' text. A trip is a break, his thalamus told him. The trees of the woods they passed were green, a green so evidently different from the green of the meadows. Difference and resemblance at the same time! Strange … 'Perhaps we should have lunch at the 'Blue Boar'?', Llewellyn asked. 'Good idea!', Omega remembered a rather dark and cosy room, several wooden tables, a silent drunkard – probably – at the bar.

Soon they were sitting at one of these tables. Their two steaks were approaching, carried by a nice young waitress, country style, friendly. Llewellyn said that he was working on a problem, a serious problem. It had nothing to do with his job, he was a high school teacher, a math teacher. Nothing had to do anything with his job. That was the nice thing with his job, it was so far away from any relevance, math itself could do the teaching. It was 'cool' like the temperature in the fridge. And during teaching no research takes place, 'teaching math is like sleeping.', he explained. No, his serious problem was rather emotional. Or, more precisely, rational-emotional. Omega noticed that Llewellyn did not want to say what the problem actually was. It seemed that he just wanted to play a language game: Sneak around in approximate circles, never revealing where the center of your irregular language movements really is. Confuse your audience with transitory spirals that quickly turn into explosions. Omega suddenly realized that this game was not under Llewellyn's control. It was taking place within Llewellyn's head! 'I don't know what I'm missing.', Llewellyn whispered, 'Maybe not just one thing, but several things …' Omega recognized the spirals that filled the sky like appearing and disappearing stars – many spirals, indeed.

'You want to feel life, I guess.', Omega interrupted the soft moment of his friend a bit harshly. 'But you can't see it. It is invisible for you. And that's the truth: It is invisible. Because you cannot project it into words; and you only see words. You see letters and sentences dancing around and they all wonder what they are doing. What you are doing! Because these thoughts are what constitutes you, they are your substance. At least, with these thoughts you only can manifest yourself as a bundle of thoughts. Flexible, wandering bundles of thoughts – without centers. And you feel, this is not enough, I'm not content, there's a lot of sentiment missing, a whole world beyond the sea of words (for a moment Omega remembered the Sea of Holes in the Beatles movie Yellow Submarine) is promising you satisfaction – but remains invisible. Words are holes in something that they are not. So, they promise you that there is something, which they penetrate, but they do not reveal what it is!'.

Llewellyn looked exhausted. 'Let's pay.', he uttered. He was not sure if he liked Omega's sudden philosophical burst. 'Probably I need love.', he smiled mildly. 'I can't give you anything but love!', Omega knew how to play tennis – and he knew the lyrics of too many songs.

On the way back home in Omega's car, after an extended walk in the fields surrounding the 'Blue Boar', they both still smelled the scent of nature. The fields, the woods, the image of a boar, their own intimacy. Like animals. But still something invisible - something beyond friendship - was missing. Love? Without consciously formulating this question, without speaking a word, Omega shook his head and said 'No!'. Llewellyn turned his head to him and consciously misunderstanding his friend nodded: 'Yes, that's true!'.

6 BARBARELLA'S EYES

'I am still waiting for the third sexual revolution.', Barbarella looked like having said this sentence a million times. Alpha knew this sentence, it was what Barbarella said almost every morning when they met in the office. Usually, Barbarella was the first human being Alpha encountered there. She was bringing her a nice cup of coffee to her desk in the group leader room. Barbarella was Italian, the daughter of an Italian chef in a downtown restaurant. Her father had wanted her either to work in a steady job or to start an active search for a wealthy husband. She had chosen to work. Barbarella always had been fat, not disgustingly fat, but chubby, round. With fifteen she had changed her name and started to call herself Barbarella. Her real name was Eliza Minicucci, she had long dark hair, was rather small, the face heart- shaped, impressively large dark brown eyes. It was evident that she was the opposite to what her new name should signal: I am a contrast to Jane Fonda's Barbarella – discover me. Alpha liked her a lot. Against the advice of her boss – 'Never get too collegial with lower-ranked persons!' – she had invited her last month to have dinner together in a new restaurant nearby. Chat a bit, get more acquainted, get to know each other. This was when the greetings with this famous sentence was initiated. But before that happened, it was Alpha who surprised the insecure younger woman with a friendly 'You are invited, feel free to order what you want.'. Barbarella liked eating, liked it more than she wanted to – considering the shape of her belly. Eat less, but select really good food. That was what she did now. 'Thank you …', she avoided to gasp. After an hour of exploratory appetizers, they knew that this restaurant was not worth to be revisited. 'Much ado about nothing', Alpha gave her evaluation. Barbarella nodded. The conversation had turned to the usual little stories of one's family history, certain aesthetic quirks, and finally to agreements about the stupid little mistakes their boss was making. Out of the blue Barbarella said, 'In the end he is not an attractive man; I wonder if he really is married.'. 'But he wears the ring on his finger.', Alpha exclaimed – and in the same moment regretted that this was proof that she noted such signs. Barbarella hesitated, then decided to confess: 'You know, I am always looking for attractive men - with one eye at least. Most of the time I feel lonely, a bit lost. I appreciate to be entertained by the silly conversations that men start to get closer, to enable sexual intercourse. It is terrible that I share such thoughts with you, somebody I do not know at all – who is only a colleague at work. Perhaps I'm a little drunk. But I think my attitude is natural – somehow. And I feel very sympathetic to you, you know what I mean? Sex would be a good thing for me.'. She flushed - that had been too much. She had to tear her words to a more neutral, more abstract terrain. And this was when she said the ominous sentence for the first time: 'I am still waiting for the third sexual revolution.'.

Alpha had been slightly embarrassed by Barbarella's open words; now she wanted to help her in the attempt to gain neutral ground: 'What do you mean by third sexual revolution?' Barbarella happily responded with a spontaneously invented rational discourse, 'In my view, the first sexual revolution took place immediately after World War 1, in the interwar period, when the feudal rule set finally was blown up. The second sexual revolution took place in the famous sixties. Basically, a reaction to the purely growth and reconstruction-oriented hard work after the disasters of World War 2. It is a pity that I was too young to participate in this upheaval. And since the eighties we are now sliding back into an age of prudishness. This time, of course, accompanied by an excited capitalist flourishing of the porn industry. The latter pushes all sexual inclinations in an even more radical way away from fulfilment, produces even greater sexual helplessness. The discourse on sexual diversity mirrors a diversity of different kinds of loneliness. Do you see? This is why we need a third sexual revolution!'. Alpha was stupefied: 'You are an intellectual! I mean, I never assumed that you are simple – sorry – but this line of argument? Brilliant. I also will join you in your fight for the third sexual revolution!' What do I say, Alpha thought in the same moment. Are we both drunk? Barbarella reacted: 'To call someone an intellectual is a severe insult, you know my dear. Intellectual is the name of a crackpot with overflowing communication garbage.', Barbarella was happy to be on safe grounds again.

Alpha decided to order two other glasses of wine. She looked at Barbarella. 'Let us be friends.', she solemnly said. 'We are already.', Barbarella answered. It would be a long evening; they both knew it already. When Alpha finally made it into her bed – Frank was lying there, snoring – she quickly fell asleep. In her last conscious moment, she compared the face of the stranger she had seen at the train station with Frank's stupidly snoring visage. When she woke up next morning, she had forgotten this moment. What she saw when she opened her eyes were Barbarella's eyes, wide open, dark – almost black – staring at her. As if she could not believe what she saw. What did she look at? It evidently was Alpha. In this instant it was crystal clear: She – Alpha – had no personality, was without any interest for Barbarella, this was the reason why these eyes were so astonished, so open and at the same time so infinitely far away. These eyes were not disappointed, no; they never had been close, they never had aspired to come closer. The unsurmountable distance had only been bridged by alcohol, for a few hours, by lots of uncontrolled alcohol input. Was Alpha of interest for herself, for Alpha, at all? Give a damn on Barbarella, more important was her own self-esteem. She suffered. No, she only thought that she suffered, help was creeping up from the back of her consciousness: 'You can change things', this help whispered. If her life was so trite that it had destroyed her personality, then perhaps it still could be changed at any moment, she could change it. The energy stored in her, slumbering under a heap of duties and useless habits, all this energy was still there. Barbarella's eyes looking at her had provoked her to stand still, to take a deep breath and look at herself. She was alone! This sudden insight struck her like lightning. Frank was only superficial entertainment, like going to see a movie. Her job was like training in one of these boring fitness studios, endless effort for marginal improvements that lead nowhere anyway.

Probably Barbarella had experienced her eyes, Alpha's eyes, in a very similar way as what she had seen in Barbarella's glance. Barbarella was lonely too – but who cares? Barbarella was young. She looked at her finger nails. The cup of coffee that Barbarella had put on her desk was already half empty, the coffee lukewarm. Of course, the words they had exchanged this morning were more intimate, they had the common experience of last night. 'Common', what a lie? Her finger nails looked so familiar, she rarely used nail polish. More precisely, she hated nail polish. Only weakness and lazy compromises had broken this aversion a few times. Frank once had mentioned that he liked nail polish. Who is Frank? Break free – but how? This day was a long day for Alpha, she had to drown her quizzical thoughts in a busy sea of grey work activities. When she finally took the bus home, Barbarella's standard sentence jumped into her mind: 'I am still waiting for the third sexual revolution.'. This was bad news for the upcoming encounter with Frank. She was ready to leave him.

7 TRIBAL LIFE

Omega's environment, the physical and cultural conditions of his biotope, had changed a lot in the last decades. In particular, during the last five years the pace of the global climate catastrophe had been accelerating, the takeover of authoritarian regimes in all parts of the world were showing dramatic consequences: wars. He had invented a new characterisation for these regimes, he called them 'National Capitalism'. They were based on national mass media who could manipulate the internal model building schemata of the domestic population. This could not work perfectly, thus the centralised ideological manipulation had to be supplemented by increased coercive power, police and military. But even the reinforced shift towards these two political pillars of National Capitalism could not prevent that the dire economic consequences of the victory of nationalist policies, i.e., a severe fall in average global welfare, led to unrest in growing parts of the population. Pandemics, unpreceded migration waves caused by wars and climate catastrophes, and the periodically occurring breakdown of the global financial system all amplified now the instability of human life on earth. Many cultural tribes were falling apart and at the same time some new social entities, based mainly on electronic links via the internet, were forming. Omega was terrified, but also a little fascinated. What was going on out there? 'Prevent to die in a war!', seemed to be a good bottom line. It often ran counter the official war propaganda of national-capitalist regimes. It had become a popular, but dangerous slogan. In the moment, wars were still taking place in a safe distance only. But civil wars within national-capitalist regimes started to take on shape. On the periphery, best example Africa, they often were already reality. Omega would have liked to write a text that explained all these developments. It necessarily would be a sinister text – in the end the evolution of the human species was on a long-run downward movement. Perhaps the final downward movement? All life is only finite. But Omega wanted to include a cautionary vision, a hope, for a next upward development. Life wants to persist, he was convinced; the unbroken believe that at least at the level of the species life goes on, there is no death, this believe is substantial to all our activities - he thought. It is the ultimate source of what is called humanism. Omega felt an insane shiver when these slushy sentences occurred in his twisted mind. 'Sorry', he murmured. I will not write this text. 'And death is the only truly sustainable event.', his mind added as an ironical last idea to the unbearable public discourses on 'sustainability'.

'Reduce the scope', he thought. Rethink how the pincers of 'political economy' – the coercive power of politics and its opposing force of cooperative division of labour, vulgo economics – have emerged. Tell a story – he sat down at his laptop: In a small tribe the warriors dominate those who produce and reproduce what keeps the tribe biologically alive. They organise production and cultural life according to the maintenance of their power, and they justify these activities by the shelter they provide – shelter from the threats coming from neighbouring tribes.

Then, there is the general tendency that successful tribes grow, take away territory from less successful tribes and become increasingly populated. Economic activities become more diversified, overall output (now measured in money terms) grows, average welfare increases, trade flourishes. Despite occasional wars, the production framework, the economics of cooperative division of labour, expands to reach a global level. National warriors and their nationally specialised industries start to struggle for a global order that still allows them to increase their respective power as well as their respective share in profits. These national social entities are what US president Eisenhower once called the military industrial complex. It is useful to consider the two elements separately. 'Military' is still the old group of warriors. In the end, it sets the national culture, secures internal power relations and thus allows the second element, 'big industry', to expand its specialised exploitative activities. In more successful national-capitalist regimes the profits of 'industry' can trickle down to parts of the exploited classes to stimulate their nationalism, a measure that can become necessary when more warriors are needed.

Omega sighed; he did not want to delve into the details of the emergence of classical fascism. But what currently happens is an incredible shift of power away from the cooperative division of labour on the global scale, towards the national military powers of a handful of large players. It can hardly be denied that these authoritarian national-capitalist regimes carry attributes that are neo-fascist. He had arrived in the presence, at the global level of the presence, to be precise.

At the local level Omega was sitting in front of his laptop's screen. Suddenly, he was longing for company. He could not call Llewellyn; he did not want to disturb the weekly rhythm of their meetings. It would be a better solution to go to the grocery shop and buy some stuff. He knew the old lady there and could chat a little with her. And then take a walk to checkout if there are cheap offers of t-shirts on the nearby main street. He needed one, it was getting spring. He might pass by at the train station, this was almost on the way to the main street. The woman he had met on the platform was still on his mind; like a ghost that could suddenly glide down to his face and kiss him. Yes, this was a perfect plan. He saved the text file, turned off his laptop and left his apartment.

He remarked that he walked slowly, like a flaneur. Why? Perhaps, because his mind worked so fast, was so busy, wanted to spend as little energy as possible to coordinate his legs. All efforts to meet her again at the train station had failed. She might have taken a train only once; but he was sure that there was some kind of routine in her behaviour. She had been on her way to work, for sure. He passed the nearby bus station. People take trains or busses, or they use their cars. A bus was leaving the station, in one of the windows he thought to have seen her for a moment. From the back only, but with a silhouette that did fit his memories.

Oh, these memories! You cannot really control them – and that is a good thing too. They often unconsciously sort out the important things and free storage space by forgetting the garbage. So, unconsciousness plays the filter that consciousness would fail to apply. And it also purges some useless content, which my conscious behaviour in a redundant attempt to have complete galleries would have kept stored - he thought. 'What works on the level of the individual probably also works on the level of the species. We store what we have agreed to be our history, which necessarily neglects the full record of what actually happened. The history taught in schools and universities is an interpretative selection, usually chosen with a predetermined pedagogical goal. In every society standard history is a very conscious action of the currently ruling class.'. His mind had started to write a new text, 'On a global level unconsciousness enters the scene only where the ruling class starts to lose control, at the uncontrolled contradictions that the exertion of control produces. As such the social unconsciousness occurs as an unreal vision, as the hope for a different state of affairs. But being different is a very weak specification, there are infinitely many ways to be different; all but one, to be precise. As a consequence, the choice must be helped by alternative interpretations of what has happened in the past. Evidently these interpretations need to fit to the contemporary vision of the exploited classes. What they should forget – and what they will forget if contradictions hurt them hard enough – is the polemic that they are powerless and necessarily are doomed to remain so.' Then, back on earth again: Was he, Omega, doomed to never meet this woman again? No! They will meet! All attitudes that are not optimistic are wrong!

Several minutes later, at the train station, he felt lonely again. Empty train stations are not a carnival anyway, but this one was *extremely* empty just because she was not there. He bought himself a chocolate bar at a kiosk and left. It was a surprise that the afternoon then turned into a quite enjoyable shopping tour on Oxford Street again. He had to take the bus to get there, but the suburban main street would have had only amplified his solitude. 'I shop, thus I am.', Omega felt. It is the best method to lose any consciousness. To be dragged away by fashions offered, almost always fashions one dislikes. Compressed and noisy stupidness that nevertheless works as an embedding aquarium providing consolidation. Forgetting due to noise nowadays is the standard procedure for forgetting. The particles dance their Brownian motion – day and night long. It was already getting dark when Omega took the bus to go home.

In the bus he became a bit afraid of entering his apartment again. His text was waiting there. First, they would ignore each other, but soon the text would call him: 'I am waiting! Where are you?'. Omega would not react immediately, 'I can kill you with a few keystrokes, you know.'. But he still liked his text, a little bit at least. Late in the night he sat down at the screen again. Tomorrow I will spend some time at the bus station, he said to himself before he started to write. I am almost sure that she usually takes the bus to go to work.

8 RAMONA

Frank was happy when he sensed that Alpha will leave him. First, that surprised him, but at second thought he found that he always knew that their relationship was not deep enough to last a whole life. So, the story of Frank and Alpha collapsed, actually it was Frank who collapsed. The rest of his life was of no interest – even for Frank himself. Though luckily, he did not even recognize it. He was just another standard fate.

Alpha changed to a new apartment, which she easily could afford due to her savings as group leader. She loved it to select new furniture, to discover the new shops nearby – the new apartment was closer to her office. She also bought several new clothes. In all of her actions not a single thought on Frank popped up. He had disappeared without leaving a trace. She went out in the early evening, had a look at her smartphone to check if there was a movie she would like to see. Or, she stayed at home cooked a nice dinner with the things she had fetched from the supermarket, some well-chosen music in the background. Life was easy, at least in the first two months after Frank's exit. Then something deeply disturbing happened.

Alpha broke her leg. She had been a bit late in the morning and was rushing down the steps from her apartment in the second floor. Her left foot was not completely in her shoe, only the toes were dragging it. After the third step she stumbled, wanted to catch the shoe again with her foot but failed, lost her balance and fell. In most cases such an incidence only leads to some bruises, but Alpha had bad luck. The moment she was lying there, she immediately knew that her right leg, with which she had tried to manage a soft landing, was broken; some ten centimeters below her knee a fierce pain signaled it. Shit! A man she did not know yet, probably a neighbour from the third floor, appeared only a minute later. She still was lying there, shocked and softly whimpering. He helped her back in her apartment, called a doctor that he knew. The rest was routine.

In the hospital her broken leg received the standard treatment. Of course, she hated her plastered leg. Her new freedom had received a severe blow. On the other hand, she only had to go to her office twice a week; her boss had agreed to let her do her work in home office mode for the next three weeks. Barbarella was helping her, was going shopping and visited her regularly. At home she now had plenty of time to '*reinvent herself*', as she had started to call her new start. Her life, the daily routines, had come to a halt. Had to change completely, would be different after three weeks, she decided. The insignificance of Frank is teaching me a lesson, she thought. I do not want to be like Frank, I want to leave my mark in life, I now have the urgent wish to extend my self-esteem. I probably always had it, but it was buried beneath a heap of ridiculous pseudo-goals and stupid monkey business. Now I will look out for my serious talents, for my place in society - and for real fun.

The moment she formulated these sentences, she already felt that this was cheap talk, cheap talk to herself. Only the part with the real fun seemed to be easily manageable. She developed a new hobby: In the evening she often watched old black & white movies on TV. These early cinematic master pieces had simple plots, actors were usually exaggerating a lot, the subtly manipulating tricks of contemporary movie producers were absent. The suggested style was no style, it was just pure black and white, around the middle of the 20th century. What got her started was a silly little video on YouTube: The Beatles with the song 'Besame Mucho' in 1962, in black & white. This was from where they started their career; and 1962 was ten years before she was born. 'Go back to the roots', she thought, 'Rediscover your character; what was the revolt; what is your revolt?'.

Stupid songs about kisses and love. She found another jewel, originally from 1928, more stumbled than sung and strangely alienated into jazz by Louis Armstrong: Ramona. The men singing, the men longing for kisses and love. Of course, the deeply engrained cultural focus on patriarchal dominance had men in the foreground. Even if a woman was staged – like Josephine Baker or later Marylin Monroe – it was just a male projection of a wish for an imagined female creature. At least in the world of black & white movies women remained unreal constructs. Nevertheless, these constructs fascinated her, they fascinated her like the strange female name 'Ramona'. Artificial, somehow southern, Italian perhaps, maybe Spanish? Not a human being of flesh and blood. She thought about a Torero, an allegory of machismo, dancing the Tango, throwing his female partner away in disgust and dragging her close to his chest in the next moment. The male actor torn apart by his feelings and using – only using – the woman as a physical counterpart of his psychotic dance.

She loved these black & white movies because she was not part of them. No female role model, no highly intelligent – but beautiful – female secret service agent, no extremely strong street-fighting woman saving poor families. Simply, nobody resembling Alpha could be found there. It was profoundly relaxing to watch them. She looked at her plastered leg, then took a pencil and in very small letters wrote 'I love you'. She smiled about the twofold irony: She hated the inconvenient plastered leg, but she loved herself; and somebody reading the words would probably think that there was somebody else writing this message to her, which then would imply an immediate message to the reader too.

For her dancing the Tango, being a Ramona, was out of reach – at least in the moment; with this plastered leg. But more important also because she was feeling that she was made of flesh and blood, that her life had reached a point where she needed to step out into her true existence. The doorbell was ringing, Barbarella was bringing fresh fruits, milk, butter, some yoghurt and bread. She smiled and evidently was looking forward to distribute the latest office gossip. It took Alpha a moment to switch gear, a strange sentence tried to take hold in the back of her brain: 'It takes two to Tango!'. But Barbarella was pitiless and started with her stories before she did close the door. It turned out that half of the things she had brought were planned to be eaten together with Alpha, a common snack in the late afternoon.

9 THE EYE OF A HURRICANE

Again, the geopolitical level: What will happen next? In the next ten to twenty years, say? Omega hesitated. He had forgotten where his line of argument had stopped. Had it really been his argument? Or was it the text itself, which was growing out of its internal logic; using him, Omega, only as an external writing device? Like an old-style typewriter that did not store letters, words and sentences, which had forgotten what just has been printed the moment you withdrew your finger, just like this machine he had forgotten the paragraphs he had written a few hours before when he had left his apartment. It *definitely* was the text that kept on moving, was ensuring that the dynamics of the argument were there, did not stop to proceed. He was the instrument of the text. And he had been standing still for a few hours, had needed a break. The instrument had to be put on a rest, had to be sent to spend some leisure time to reload its batteries. Now the instrument was back, but to be applied again it had to be re-initiated. It had acquired new energy, but this energy was looking around in its momentary, immediate surroundings and did not see in which direction to go. It had lost its memory. And that is a sure sign that it – that he - indeed was the text's instrument: Instruments tend to lose their memories, example typewriter! To keep them and to use them for pattern recognition and action adaption according to these pattern interpretations was the trick behind the fashion of so-called *machine learning*.

Omega was a less sophisticated instrument. He just could read the last few paragraphs of his text to get into motion again. Memories are the catalysts starting the upswing of my text's waves. Once they are activating my brain cells these little devils make the text going. Then the interaction is in its flow. It is pouring the text into the keyboard and almost simultaneously on the screen. Just until at an unforeseeable moment the process suddenly stops; without warning the flow ends, the channel is mute. I have to stand up and leave, even too exhausted to hope that it will start again when I return. These are these strange and highly asymmetric text waves. In a sense they resemble the asymmetric waves of attraction and rejection between a woman and a man. The role of the instrument might change from time to time – but a Tango wave persists. The image of the pair dancing an Argentinian Tango did not go away easily as he tried to read the last two paragraphs of his text. Then he started again.

Eisenhower, he thought: *Born in 1890 and being an active element of the military industrial complex of the US during World War 2, he nevertheless warned from the over boarding power of this complex in 1961. He had been in the center – supreme commander of Allied Forces in Europe - of the most violent battles of the largest war in human history. After the war as president of the USA, during the so-called Cold War, he sensed that mankind just moved along, he, the president, sitting in the eye of a hurricane. The next world war easily could wipe out the whole species. Eisenhower died in 1969, but the growth of power of the military industrial complex continued. It continued in the USA and in the Soviet Union, in China and in the larger European States. It was kept in check by an unprecedented growth of the global division of labour that allowed for tranquilizing subsidies for the exploited classes in the centers of capital accumulation. No world war since 1945, somehow still thinking – and slowly forgetting - to be in the eye of the hurricane, the following generations in the better-off states got used to look only at their local environment. Only the military elite of the most powerful players never lost sight of the ultimate goal of every military conflict: namely to destroy the enemy. After Mao Zedong's death in 1976 (Stalin had already died in 1953) China's development took a route that diverged markedly from the one taken by Stalin's followers in the Soviet Union. China stepwise embraced more and more economic practices copied from Western market economies, while at the same time strengthening the links between military, party political and regional governance leaders. This allowed for stronger surveillance plus a remarkable increase of the average welfare of the Chinese population. In contrast, the Soviet Union put all its economic and scientific force in the support of its weapons industry, the part of the economy dearest to the military elite. Its contribution to the advancing global division of labour remained its rich reservoir of energy sources: oil and gas. The deal with the Soviet Union's satellite states in Eastern Europe was to deliver cheap energy in exchange for the somewhat more advanced manufactured goods produced there. In the end the unsatisfactory living standards in the Eastern European satellite states – television suddenly made this visible for the broad public in the East – together with the maintenance of rigid police (and military) intervention, keeping democratic participation at a minimal level, lead to the collapse of the Soviet Union in 1990. US-led NATO could advance to Eastern Europe. In Russia the economic elite of a new group, the oligarchs, seemed to take over. Actually, they did not stay on Russian territory but spread all over the world. To keep their profits exploited on Russian grounds they had to keep good relationships with the Russian military elite. Nevertheless, the ties between Russia oligopolists and its military elite weakened. Around the beginning of the new millennium the Russian military elite consolidated its supremacy and streamlined its leadership. Several oligarchs, staying mainly abroad, started out for independent economic adventures. Also, China began to become a major hub for the global production network during the first decade of the new millennium. Remarkably, China's entry point to the global production system concerned not only real physical production processes and trade of their products, it also concerned global finance. China's exchange rate policy and the acquisition of US government bonds showed that China was aspiring to become a major player in global finance. The great financial crisis of 2008, during which China suffered much less than the West, made clear that China had arrived as the major rival to US hegemony.*

Omega stopped typing. Though he was convinced that the arguments in the text were correct, he nevertheless knew that they contained several speculative elements. One thing he was sure of was that the text should not go into more detail. He had to warn the text: You will lose readers, the details will eat you up, you will never be finished. He knew these dangers from the time when he wrote his PhD thesis. In the end he had to use a completely inappropriate ending just to meet the date when he had to deliver his thesis - very unsatisfactory. A few months after he had finished his parents both died in a car crash. This had changed his life dramatically. All over sudden he had inherited a large sum of money – but was almost alone. No other relatives, just a group of friends, students of his age, no girlfriend, but rather wealthy for his age. Llewellyn, of course, his best friend, who became his anchor man. He sold the house of his parents – after the terrible accident it was impossible for him to live there – and bought an apartment closer to the city. He now owned enough money, actually assets, to avoid to find a steady job. The monthly payment derived from his wealth was good enough to lead a convenient middle-class life. And so – out of the blue – he had decided to become a writer, an author of texts of his choice. He first wanted to finish at least two books before he would dare to approach a publishing house. At that time, he did not know that it would be the text that would guide him, would subordinate him as its instrument. Now, with the first book almost finished, the question of finding a publisher was losing its importance. Writing now was dancing, the stop-and-go-and-stop-and-go, the wave that drove his life.

Only the face of the woman on the platform at the train station had broken the soft rhythm of his life. When she suddenly reappeared in his mind, he felt that he could not continue with the text. Not now – probably later. There was an acquaintance between his relationship to the text and his link to this unknown woman. He wanted to be close to her, to be her instrument, to be soaked up by her, to be loved by her. And at the same time, he was afraid of all that, she implicitly had to push him away to maintain his wonderful longing for her. A wavelike motion, a dance, again. In the moment – sitting in front of the screen that starred at him – neither the text nor the woman owned him. He was frozen in the eye of the two overlapping hurricanes.

Not too far away from Omega's apartment Alpha finally had said goodbye to

Barbarella and was returning to her sofa to watch the news. She was not too interested in consuming these filtered glimpses on what TV imperia thought to be important; 'important' and manipulating, meeting marketing tasks anyway. Television always is a one-way channel: They choose what is 'important' and how they transmit their interpretations of what they want you to think is the larger reality. Considerable parts of their interpretative force they sell to private firms for polluting your eyes and ears with their rubbish. Other parts go to political entrepreneurs, people whom the media owners think to be useful to provide them some tax money and a convenient juridical environment. Why did she enter this shower cubicle of TV information at all? Well, there were not too many peepholes into the world outside her local environment. Yes, there was the internet with its social media channels. But in this chaotic mess the same – and even worse – media moguls were reigning. It was difficult to find valid information, information with the slight bias that she preferred, that reflected her own – always preliminary - position. She kept starring at the TV screen. Then, in a sudden change of mood she turned the TV set off, put the remote control on the sofa and decided to take a walk. Not now though, as a glimpse on her plastered leg reminded her. It was already dark outside, around 10 pm. All these false news, all these brewing up catastrophes – illusionary and real ones – knocking at the door of her attention, all that found her standing calm in the middle of her living room. Alpha felt strong. She still could not run, but next week the plaster would be gone, she could go for a short walk around the block. For now, she still remained the unmovable eye in the middle of a hurricane.

Omega walked down the narrow street in front of his apartment. At the corner he turned left. He had a plan: Next Street turn right, then turn left, then right again; then turn left twice, pass straight over three crossroads, stop there and check how far away from home you are. Then return home. A perfect plan! Of course, Omega knew what Brownian motion and what Wiener processes are - he once even had been interested in Levy Flights – but for now he was lazy and took a short-cut: Omega wanted to be surprised by the location where he would land and for that purpose his simple planning decisions were good enough. 'Free will' as scarce and as stupid as can be, indeed a signum of free will.

He ended up at a crossroad of two streets he did not know. Blocks of buildings had had very different sizes, the lengths between corners varied a lot. Midnight was approaching, he was positively surprised that at the corner of the two streets the lights of a pub promised that it was still open – no more alcohol, of course. He entered the 'Iron Maiden Saloon' and sat down at the bar. The barkeeper, visibly a fan of the heavy metal group in the name of the pub, grinned friendly but warned that they will close soon. Omega nodded, asked for a coke and had a look at google maps on his smartphone. Only a 30 minutes' walk to his apartment! Strange that he never had been in this place. Back at home he was tired and went to bed.

Before he fell asleep, he thought he should repeat a random walk like this one as soon as possible.

10 THE SEA

Alpha loved sea waves. During school holidays her parents always spent two weeks with her in a cheap little hotel in Italy. As a young child she spent every single day of these holidays on the beach, mainly in the water, to be precise. Head above the waves, sometimes a slow jump to stay clear from the salty taste of a breaking wave, feeling the sand between the toes – underwater. Later, when she learned that the waves are not horizontal movements of water but a result of the coordinating forces of its vertical movements, she was wondering how such a complicated internal system had been translated in her superb feeling of a girl swaying freely in this elementary medium. My body certainly is still the result of endless evolutionary turns and waves of water, or of even more basic beginnings. Oxygen, hydrocarbons, what kind of waves? Chemistry at school was not one of her favourite subjects, teachers were bad and uninterested. To love sea waves, it was not necessary to understand their emergence, their dynamics. But underneath her love there was something hidden, a kind of secret interest. If she remembered the days of her youth well, then the most exciting experiences were to dive into a breaking wave. What exactly happened in the breakpoint moment remained always a surprise.

Perhaps there had not been enough surprise in her life as an adult, she now thought. There had been waves, of course: The life at school, the days as a student, the days of a young professional before Frank, the life with Frank. A bit like the vertical movements of water molecules in sea waves, rather straight forward but mostly unaware of any horizontal movement. Driven by the interplay of the forces exerted by neighbouring water molecules, in a sense caught by this kind of network structure into which your birth had thrown you. Only an arbitrary sudden action could lead her out of this cage, she thought, only an unexpected turn could revive this breakpoint moment that the young girl had loved so much. She still was in the eye of the hurricane – frozen, almost motionless - but only for one more week. After this week something fundamental had to happen, she was sure of herself. Though she had no idea what this something would be. She would throw herself into the violent outer spirals of the hurricane. Maybe they would transport her to the surface of the sea, where she could breathe freely, see the horizontal waves, experience the full picture, horizontal combined with vertical. Maybe.

Water was a very special fluid. As salty sea water it provided sea waves - pure well-being for body and eyes - and inhibited drinking it. As cool sweet water it was the archetype of drinking – pure refreshment, support for continuous survival. And she was just a tiny molecule of that stuff? No, not of that stuff, she had inertia. It might have been the case that most of the time she had been swaying around as the innocent result of myriads of influences from all directions. But evolution produces a direction, produces asymmetries, produces time. 'And the times they are changing', sang Robert Zimmermann.

They are not changing like simple waves, like harmonic waves, she suddenly recognized. They change with a sawtooth pattern: They are the *breaking* waves!

The surfers of monster waves. How do they feel when they are on top of such a wave, on a zenith of silence shortly before they go down so fast, so steeply amidst the chaos of falling water? Water again.

She had one more week. Her heart was beating, she felt some excitement. But just some … A few minutes later she slept.

Again, the young girl Alpha; the molecule raising its head out of the wet mass of neighbouring molecules. She could see, look over the surface of the sea, could see the horizon! The horizon was a straight line. And as she saw it, she knew already that it was not a straight line; that it was just a band of waves; that it was only her limited perception capability that produced this illusion of a straight line. As always in life: There is no straight line outside of your head, but straight lines – linear relationships as her math teacher would have called them – are the main device with which brains start to work. Imitation is a linear relationship steering the behaviour of animals, including humans. Nevertheless, our physical environment unceasingly teaches us how straightness is the wrong assumption, or at least only a first bad approximation. Even gravitation between bodies decreases with the square of the distance between them. As a single molecule deep down in the sea she had experienced the chaos, the loss of individual direction and free will, the life as an uncontrollable mass of water. Water again.

But now, soon, at the end of this week, she would have reached the highest point of a wave. The point from where she could see clearly where the horizon was, where she could choose a direction. Of course, there was always a finite – even a rather limited - set of possible directions in life. But that was okay as long as it did not shrink to just one possibility. Probability was a concept that always had confused her: It was the attempt to nail down knowledge of non-knowledge. The strange thing was that the new probabilistic knowledge on non- knowledge did not completely eat up all of the non-knowledge. If you knew that each side of a perfect dice could come up with a probability of one sixth, you still could surprise yourself by actually rolling the dice. There is no big difference in surprise if the five comes up and you started with the expectation that this time it must be a three, or that you started with the expectation that the three has a probability of one sixth. And it doesn't matter at all if you record all past outcomes, the surprise persists.

What were here possible choices, what was her finite set of actions? This was an important question, Alpha thought. With her choice she would defeat probability, would devaluate all but one of the possible choices – a collapse of the probability function as her teacher would have formulated it. The question had to be split in two parts, she recognized. The first part was to find all feasible actions, the second part was to ascribe the consequences and impact on her of each of the possible actions. The two steps depended on each other. If an alternative implicated an overwhelming influence of negative impacts, then further investigation could be skipped. On the other hand, the imagination of what could provide a substantial positive impact could help to discover an alternative that at first glance had been overlooked.

Alpha sighed, dry methodological stuff; probability considerations would not help her much. What where her alternatives anyway? As everybody else she was caught in a network of monetary dependencies: Earn the money that you need for living, and be glad if a few hours per day remain to recover for the next working day. This basic circuit would not change much if she would move to a different job. She would remain a powerless molecule in an omnipotent sea. Why bother about alternatives? But wait! She could work part time; in the end with a well-paid job and a reduction of expenses she might at least get half of their lifetime for her own disposal. Half of life! What should I do with that offer? Five or six choices sprang immediately into her mind. All of them daring, all of them promising. But somehow – each one rather 'unrealistic', illusionary. They were lighthouses at the horizon that the molecule Alpha could barely identify. But these promises were possible complements, accommodating half-life, which signaled that existence needs opposing elements. And it is her, Alpha, to decide on the direction that the working contradiction of her future will take; in which valleys and on which mountains it will aim. The waves are waiting for her, they won't stop, never. She felt tired, exhausted without any specific reason.

Later, in her bed, an old song was playing in the radio. She always had loved this song: 'Let it ride' by Chi Coltrane. No jazz, despite the father of Chi, John Coltrane; or probably because of him. And this song gave her the distance to fall asleep – let it ride.

In her dream she was sitting quietly at a beach watching the waves, their repeating disappearance, transformation into the gentle licking on the wet sand. Almost an eternal reminder of eros, a contrast to the stoic horizon that had sent them. She smiled with eyes firmly closed. The art of waiting for your own decision, a perfect image of this art.

11 THE NIGHT

Omega was awake, it was dark outside. The night is the time when the rotating earth turns away from the sun. I am sitting on this enormous ball of mixed material; I trust that it keeps on turning. It is 10 pm, the night has started. We need the night. Omega went to his little table that stood in front of the window, the table with the laptop. He sat down and stared out of the window. Not into the dark, of course, but just on the front of other windows on the opposite side of the street. A panopticon of living stories hidden behind lighted and dark rectangles. He opened his laptop, then – abruptly – hesitated.
Think first, he thought, smiling about the double entry of the verb. He thought he should think, though he already thought exactly that. You cannot think not to think! It's plain like that, flat as a pancake. Nights are there because movements are not straight, movements mostly are rotations; even stranger: exploding or imploding spirals. The verb returns to the verb, but later and with a different colour. And in somewhat regularly reoccurring, narrow intervals the body of the rotating mass hinders the sun to shine in me – it is night. My perceptive abilities with respect to the outside world are restricted, my thoughts are forced to dance their Tango inside my head. It is clear: While you dream your body is not moving too much, this provides room for your dreams to go wild. Boring dreams are rare, and you're protected by forgetting them instantly. The most fruitful times are the transition periods shortly before and after dreaming. When freely floating associative forces build-up, or are trying to land in the morning light. In my personal experience the night is not dark at all, Omega thought. It rather is a reminder that the outside is an outside. Make it less visible and you see how its reflections form your inside, you experience a double inside. And not just one mirror image is grafted on your consciousness, there often are four or five illusionary pictures waiting for you. No, not pictures; movies, short films. And if

it is early morning, if the day breaks, then you would be ready to share this flood of experiences - Omega! But only for a few seconds, then you're so accustomed to forgetting them that you do not really recognize that you did so. Omega – the last letter of the alphabet - nothing follows, just empty and timeless space. The night is over, colours vanish and other colours, essentially different colours are awaking. Where has this strange feeling - this yearning of the first seconds of the new day - gone? It is still looming in you – Omega – it is the floor on which you walk during daylight. You are looking for somebody. Maybe, this somebody is not just you again. Does it take two to tango?

Omega looked at his watch, it was ten minutes after ten. 'The sun and the rotation of the earth structure what we experience as time.', he started a new piece of text. 'The seasons as well as day and night frame our experiences. We are built on these foundations. Repetition is the frame of our perception; we recognize what is repeating - is the same, on the background of a new day, a new season. Experience just is a processing contradiction between 'same' and 'different'. We live along many days and many seasons till we finally disappear. How long we live is a third measure; a measure, which has roots in the species we belong to. Average lifetime is something that only makes sense if there is a population of a species that allows for averaging. This third measure thus leads directly to the mystery of the emergence of life. The only law of physics that involves time is the second law of thermodynamics, which tells us that in the long-run all order is destroyed – or: the final order is complete randomness. Luckily this law is a *probabilistic* law, meaning that it is possible that during a certain period order increases, i.e., life emerges, ordered self-organizing structures can maintain themselves and eventually even grow for days, for years. But at the same time this probabilistic nature implies that that life is necessarily finite; sooner or later order – we - must die. The fact of general finiteness can be taken easy if we look back to our birth. No problem that there was a time when we did not exist. Looking forward to our death, finiteness is harder to swallow. For this case humans developed humanism, meaning that the survival of the species provides some comfort if the individual exit approaches. The third measure accompanies this substitution of an individual fate by a species' perspective: We maintain a double consciousness. The average of eighty years, which individuals living in the rich part of the world currently can expect for their life span, this average reflects the ability to maintain a common consciousness, a species consciousness, within each individual entity. Because the individual life-span is much shorter than the species' life-span the idea of humanism makes sense. Even if it sometimes contradicts individual desires. To live with this unavoidable contradiction, to thrive on the thrills it produces, becomes possible by splitting our time in episodes – shorter chunks of conscious behaviour pointing in more or less opposing directions.'

Omega hesitated. There was no evident next sentence. He felt lost and leaned back. Staring at the screen did not help. His guideline had been to explore the night, to explore the concept behind the night, behind the episode 'night'.

And now he got stuck. 'The night – close your eyes – the night.', Omega thought. And indeed, he closed his eyes. With closed eyes in front of his laptop he was astonished that his world was not black, not even dark. It was grey! Grey is the colour of randomness. Out of unconscious uniform grey, shades of grey emerge, contrasts of entities become visible. All at once they jump into the mind of the sleeper, the sleeper he now was. These entities were now extremely colourful, loaded with memories from past daytimes, though mixed-up and shifted into exciting transformations. That was all he knew when after a few minutes he abruptly woke up again. There was an in-built mechanism in dreaming, a switch that deletes memories of dreams shortly after the wake-up. Maybe the evolution of the species has formed this switch because that is exactly the characteristic function of dreaming: to forget. To forget, to erase memories, to start anew with a cleaned-up storage in your brain. Of course, not all is forgotten. But the remaining memories appear in new clothes, are re-dressed.

'*The night is an episode of reshuffling, of dancing with your old memories to create a new existence.*', Omega wrote this next sentence of his text. He liked his sentence, and felt a bit ashamed of his vanity. But to forget indeed was something that was essential in life, in his life, in everybody's life. And it was not common sense to perceive forgetting as work, mostly it was seen as a deficiency. Nevertheless, evolution had selected forgetting as a valuable trait. We all sleep. He saw that he had unconsciously had touched the keyboard so his text's words now appeared in italics.

'*Being reborn every morning is a mysterious experience, which itself mysteriously is not appreciated too often, is taken as self-evident, is forgotten. The night as an episode of partial non-existence is taken for granted. If you go out in the evening, spend the night with friends in bars and discotheques, drinking and dancing, eventually having sexual adventures, then you are substituting your dreams with some free-wheeling time-out from ordinary life. Or, at least, you try to do so. The night is grey, and if you live it instead of closing your eyes, then the emerging contours might be as boring and clueless as dreamless unconsciousness.*'

Again, he stopped writing and looked at his watch: 10.30. He should go out, he thought. The possibility of conscious unconsciousness attracted him. At second thought it was irresistible. The escape from his apartment just took ten minutes. Then he was in the grey streets again, wondering which direction he should take. Nothing was completely unknown, but everything was only shades of grey. His eyes were taking photographs while he turned his head to different sides. Then his feet started walking without any order from his brain – a feeling of relieve pervaded his mind. His body could take care of him, and it did. Getting lost was like going home. Of course, he knew that he could reconstruct the way he had taken – no problem. But he would not; he had decided to forget as good as he could. Grey veils, in short. The night was warm, was it a San Francisco night – he heard Eric Burden's song in the back of his brain. Was Burden still alive? Were we still alive? At the corner of two streets with no shops and no other people around he stopped and looked around. All these rectangular blocks of indifferent houses, all these dreams taking place in these dwellings, all this incredible amount of permanent forgetting taking place – he sighed. He sat down on the pavement, like a fearless but tired animal. Then he saw someone coming round the next corner of the darker street. He quickly stood up not to give the impression of being drunk – or in need for help. No contact, please. The night belongs to me. '… and my monkey.', whispered a forgotten singer in his head. The other man passed by, looking straight ahead, murmuring something, slightly shaking his head a bit. Omega continued. Continued to breath, continued to exist, continued to walk.

A strange feeling creeped up his back while he randomly chose one of the three streets. The feeling could not be expressed in a single word, it needed a sentence: 'The night is too long.'. 'Yes, feelings are sentences!', this sudden discovery struck him from behind. And since the mixture of feelings is one of the pillars of thought processes our very existence is built on a strange brew of more or less arbitrary sentences. The arsenal of hidden memories in the Thalamus, of course, was a second pillar that accommodates the purely physical set of signals coming from our environment, from our borderline. The skin, my borderline, has border crossings - eyes, ears, the sense of smell – that help to define my position relative to all the world that is not me. And, yes, I am always a mover in a double sense: relative to my outside environment and also internally, relative to these strange heaps of sentences that constitute me.

Then Omega saw them, the letters that were still lightened to signal that the location was still open: *Iron Maiden Saloon*. Something he could aim at, almost a reason for living.

Alpha could walk again, still a bit slower than before her accident, but she could. She stepped out into the night and immediately felt incredibly free. The fresh air becomes my aura, she thought, and had to giggle because she never had understood what exactly an aura should be. An accessoire like a shiny new pair of earrings? But now she had it, whatever it was! She decided that her plan was to proceed by alternating the sequence of decisions: turn left, go straight ahead, turn right. Stop after an hour and try to get back by inverting the last decision and then using the sequence: straight ahead, turn right, turn left. A perfect plan with some in- built randomness and nevertheless a good chance to get close to her home again. It was her plan and it promised the correct dose of fun and stubbornness, which her future life should deliver. After half an hour she was standing at the crossroads in front of the '*Iron Maiden Saloon*'. The plan said 'turn right!', but a strong feeling in Alpha said 'No, turn left to the entry of the saloon!'. She tried to rationalize where this feeling came from. No idea, no sentence jumped into her mind. Actually, she never had liked the band Iron Maiden, this was stupid heavy metal. Perhaps it was her new aura, to decide really without borderlines, to decide against her own decisions. She entered the saloon. There were only two men. If she was Eve carrying an apple, she now would have to decide whom to give the apple. One of the two men clearly was a barkeeper. She turned to him and with a firm voice ordered a coke. But then she turned to the other guy that was sitting at the table in the corner and gave him the apple: 'May I join you?'. She sat down opposite to him, smiling a bit shy. Omega stared at Alpha. What was going on here? After five seconds he was able to answer: 'Yes, please. What a surprise! I know you … from the bus … some time ago …'. In the same moment Alpha realized that her behaviour in the saloon had not been random at all. Her body must have identified the guy long before her consciousness now found out who he was. He must have inhabited her mind for weeks. They both celebrated this saint moment with a minute of silence.

Then Alpha's new activist turn broke through: 'I think, I like you; I really like you!'. Omega was taken away, leaned forward, and right across the table took her hand. To feel the skin of her hand electrified him in a way that he had to hide – calm down, don't destroy this sensation. 'And I have been waiting for this moment for weeks.', he stumbled. Then time speeded up.

They all but were unable to notice how fast they paid and left the Iron Maiden Saloon, holding each other tight out on the street.

In between the high apartment buildings down the street, there was an empty space that had been filled with a really small park. A little green with a few small trees, a sandbox and three park benches. It looked like the hole of a lost tooth in the line of the middle-aged row of buildings. During the day there would be a handful of mothers and fathers of small children glad to use this retreat. But now – during the night – it was rather dark. A single lamppost at the entry spread a weak illumination, the second lamppost inside the park did not work. Alpha and Omega quickly decided; they headed – almost rushed - for this park. Alpha took the initiative. In the next moment Omega was sitting on one of the benches where Alpha had placed him. Alpha got rid of her slip - fortunately, she had decided to wear a skirt today, she freed Omega's penis from its hideaway. Then she spread her legs and sat down on him. In the millisecond before penetration, she wondered how close to sexual nudity she always is during daytime. They immediately fell into trance and in a mind-blowing rhythm both came three times in a row.

As Omega recovered from this extra-terrestrial experience, he felt blind and clairvoyant at the same time. What a woman? How to live on a lower level on lust than what just had happened. He looked at Alpha as she was settling down, finding her slip, pulling up her slip, arranging her skirt, closing her blouse. Without him inside her she probably felt as empty as he – they both had given all of them to their unification. Unification - such a stupid word. Almost as stupid as the word sex. Words and sentences necessarily failed to describe what he nevertheless stored in his memory as the primordial experience.

A few minutes later they left the park. Omega accompanied Alpha home, holding hands, speaking little, being content to smile, to conserve a little bit of trance. At the door to the staircase Alpha remembered to exchange telephone numbers, in case …. And a quick agreement to meet tomorrow in the evening, say eleven, at the Iron Maiden Saloon again. Finally, a passionate kiss. Passionate, though both were aware that this kind of passion is only a far cry from what they had shared – had multiplied - on the park bench. A kiss, a nice little placeholder to remember what true passion could be like. Later they both lied in their beds waiting to fall asleep. A sweet sleep this time. The night was gone, was dissolved into omnipresent satisfaction.

12 BLUE MEANIES

The next morning Alpha woke up with the decision to keep her workplace, to go to the office as if nothing special had happened. It suddenly appeared to be a straightforward rational decision: The night had turned into her daytime, her real life, the arena where all her wishes promised to become true. On the opposite side, her daytime was just a dream, a shallow and uninteresting dream. It was a good thing if it did not bother her too much, this was leaving time for reverse 'daydreaming', leading to a minute of real life in her head while she was staring at a computer screen.

It took a few weeks till the mild disturbances of her reverse daydreaming became somewhat nastier. In the first week, she was meeting Omega every night. The rain was forcing them more often to give up their park bench and use one of their two apartments. Of course, they now had also spent a lot of time telling each other their respective life stories. While this certainly completed their mutual awareness of who the other was, having sex still remained the central element of their meetings. 'This is real life!', Alpha thought.

Then a new boss, actually only a new division manager, changed the well-established workflow she had got used to. Her workload almost doubled as the new boss tried to excel by saving wage costs, firing one of her colleagues. Instead of doubling her salary, he rather repeatedly used the example of the unhappy ex-colleague to put pressure on her. It could easily be also her fate to be fired. Secretly, Alpha called him a Blue Meanie – like the enemies of the Beatles in the movie Yellow Submarine. This Blue Meanie increasingly became hard to stand. Today's Blue Meanies are not comic, are not disguised as clowns – though intellectually they usually are. They should wear brown shirts, like Hitler's followers, she thought. But their actual disguise now was the 'slim-fit idiot'. Not every man wearing a slim-fit suit was a 'slim- fit idiot', she admitted. Some of them were just idiots - like the average crackpot, whose outfit she did not even notice. She was sure that her boss would have liked to start an affair with her, and that it was the impossibility – his knowledge of this impossibility – that produced his hardly concealed hate. Her natural accomplice in her battle against the boss was Barbarella. As a simple secretary – and a less attractive woman - Barbarella was far below the radar of the boss. So first he was surprised when many of the simple duties of secretaries, like the coffee they prepared for him or the newspapers they put on his desk in the morning before he arrived, turned worse, became needle pricks irritating and disturbing his daily routines. They were too minor to be punished, but they were many. The game Alpha and Barbarella played against him clearly was soon the major topic when they had a quick coffee after work. Alpha's battleground was her occasional meeting with the boss's boss, one of the owners of the firm. She knew him from the early times when she was the rising young star in the firm. Her subtle critique of the Blue Meany was appreciated, the owner never did wear a slim-fit suit. His broad grey trousers and his worn-out old jacket – though supreme quality – signaled his preference for convenience. It was a companion on the board of the firm who had hired the new division manager to boost profits.

As time went by these stupid little games in her work life more and more lost their innocence of irrelevant, though annoying, dreams. She talked to Omega about it. Omega looked serious and murmured, 'I know'. 'Did you ever read Adorno?', he added. 'I know the name, but – frankly – never have read anything.'. Omega continued: 'Does not matter. One of his most cited sentences is that there is no true life within a false life. A proper separation between wrong daily life and true nightlife is impossible. What is more: All elements of life change continuously and, on their way, – breaking due to their contradictions – breed new existence. Adorno was Hegelian.' Omega still looked sad. He also would have loved to continue their nightly experiences in the same unchanging strength. But he also saw its transformation coming, not only on a theoretical basis – he knew he was himself pretty much a Hegelian – but also as a slowly emerging feeling. A feeling that there is an uncertain future, which engenders hope for new areas of lust and simultaneously also a considerable package of fears.

Omega's own 'true life' was not only their nightly sex relationship. He also still lived in the text he wrote during the day. And this secondary 'true life' was getting less and less attractive. It became a kind of waiting-for-the-night. His counterpart, his missing link to be human, Alpha, had been found. He saw his primordial wish fulfilled. And now an almost philosophical idea started to emerge: There was a part of Alpha that he never would reach – a side that now became visible because they were so close! Like Kant's impossibility to reach the thing in itself, it would make Omega a stranger to Alpha. His argument - developing in the few seconds while staring at Alpha, in the back of his brain – jumped into a different field: It was like in an Argentinian Tango when the dancers in an eternal moment hold each other extremely tight and already know that in the next moment they will push each other apart. The harsh movements of their bodies accompanied by solemn, proud and self-confident faces. This latter state of affairs in his case would be underpinned by his currently disregarded text, his reason for thinking. 'Instead of living.', he added cynically and sad.

Alpha had noticed that Omega's mind was not with her any more. They were sitting in the Iron Maiden Saloon; it was eleven o'clock. 'All these Blue Meanies that surround me, in particular this Chief Blue Meanie, Venuz B. Meanie, my boss, they put up thousands of little obstacles and I have to master them. They keep me busy in a world that I do not want to be in. I think, I have to do something to overcome their attacks, I can no longer consider them as bad dreams, they take away my breath, they weaken the energy that we need. Maybe, we should fall apart a bit and I concentrate more on these minor daytime problems. Once I have done that we can unify even more, I hope.' Alpha had dared to formulate what Omega just had sensed. He admired her. She was so brave, she could go ahead, despite fears and always with an inborn light of hope. And – she was his partner in Tango dancing, solemn, proud and self-confident now. He stood up, moved to her side of the table, took her hand and dragged her in a Tango position. They started to dance in Iron Maiden Saloon a Tango to the unpleasant noise of a screamer group, which the barkeeper adored. This time they were not completely alone, there was half a dozen of aspiring young Blue Meanies watching them. They all were drunk already; it was five minutes after 11. What a scene!

No sex that night. When Omega was in his bedroom, he tried to figure out who his own Blue Meanies were. This proved to be not easy. He was a privileged individual with no troubles at a regular working place. What annoyed him? What was it that he struggled with? What did he want to overcome? His immediate answer was not satisfactory: He was fighting against vagueness. As soon as this idea was born, he knew that it was vague itself, it was ambiguous. Vagueness was never only disturbing him, it always was also the necessary ingredient that attracted him, that promised a revelation of a mystery. This double role was hardly satisfactory, because it always led to more mysteries than revelations. His Blue Meanies were an army of mysteries that were continuously changing - some disappearing, more new ones appearing behind them. He remembered that even in the Beatles movie Venuz B. Meanie in the end converted into a Beatles fan, and turned out to be an ambivalent character. Perhaps Alpha's imagined battle was inappropriate for his own situation. Omega decided to meet Llewellyn to ask him about that question. Llewellyn, the mathematician, must know more about proving vague hypotheses just to discover that new unknown territory lies behind them. Mathematics was a case of extreme coincidence of the blessings of proof and the curse of non-decidability. He tried to make an appointment with Llewellyn, called him, but did not reach him. Waves of doubt wandered through his open mind. Again, he was sitting in front of his screen. The screen displayed its text, letters and sentences, in front of his eyes, waiting for his action. Omega started to type.

I am alone in the jungle of thoughts, terribly alone. As soon as I move a few steps forward, brushing aside voluminous leaves and lianas, seeing a bit further into the future - as soon as this promises revelation, a new wave on unknown green fog falls down on me. And I shiver from fear and delight. As long as I live, I will run through this sequence again and again, I know. I even can predict some of the features of the next jungle I will dive into. But only some of them and only those in the next glade. My time horizon, my own private time horizon, has a rather limited range. Expanding it has dramatically failed in the course of my life. Now I am expecting that it contracts even faster. Now I am almost alone in time, in the present.

This was what the text told Omega. The text evidently did not know that not long-ago Alpha had discovered the concept of a horizon from a spatial perspective. Her wish to be on top of the waves corresponded to Omega's wish to look further into the future. Omega did not know Alpha's thoughts on the sea neither. Suddenly the telephone was ringing. Llewelyn was calling back. 'This is the person I want to discuss with – about time-horizons, predictions, and the lust of the loss of clarity', he thought. 'This will be the kick I need to discover the meaning of my Blue Meanies.'

Llewellyn and Omega were sitting in the Blue Boar again. Llewellyn explained: 'To predict the future two major sets of elements are necessary. First, you have to determine from where you start: What is important and can serve as an axiom, can be assumed to be known. Second, you need a set of rules, which allows you to mimic the processing of time, which tells you precisely how the set of axioms produces a possible future state of affairs. When a mathematician is trying to prove a hypothesis - which is the second core activity of a mathematician, the first core activity is to propose a hypothesis – he knows his starting point and he also knows where he wants to arrive at: a proven hypothesis. But the specific set of rules to be applied remains hidden in the dark, remains hidden in the jungle of possible rule sets. Usually, a proven hypothesis then immediately implies the prove of some other hypothesis – but still more hypothesis pop up at the horizon of a mathematician's life. The particular twist in this continuing fight for more proves is that it takes place in a completely abstract domain. Nothing outside its mathematical language can substitute its internal procedure of proving. Applying this pure mathematics to real life problems is impure. It might lead to impressive successes outside mathematics, but such applications are not mathematics proper. Platon even held that the material world follows, id est, can be derived, from the ideal world of mathematics. To be a pure mathematician still means to follow Platon.'. Omega looked serious, 'My thoughts are less rigid, I think. For truth to be explained completely within a language, to subscribe to a clear-cut set of conventions separated from the material world to receive in return a monolithic construction of true versus false - that is not the type of exaggeration I would go for. My Blue Meanies have a very material side. Their trick is that they put up the wrong contradictions to hide the more progressive contradictions.' Llewellyn broke out into laughter: 'Progressive! Did you really say progressive contradictions? Oh no! That's too much!'. Omega remained serious, a bit hurt indeed: 'Yes, progressive contradictions. Let me give an example. In bourgeoise sociology a misleading contradiction is the one between the individual and the society. It hides the progressive contradictions between the classes in a historically well-defined society. To arrive at the latter, it needs a detailed study of the respective society, and after this has found out the roots of the class struggles, then the spread of the message can lead to a change of circumstances, to a progressive revolution. Thus, the label progressive contradiction.'. Llewellyn does not want to be forced to admit that his sympathy for Platon is more religious than '*progressive*', so he waters down the issue: 'Well, in the long-run certain mathematical truths can exert a surprising influence on what becomes possible in what you call the 'real world'. Even if the motive for discovering them in the first place was purely mathematical curiosity. Take calculus! I confess that my own motivation to do science, to do mathematics, has a platonic twist. But for me this was always a question of intellectual taste. And what inspires my thrive towards knowledge acquisition is – like your dislike for vagueness – a dislike for missing pieces of the larger puzzle, which I still expect to be out there. You probably know what Paul Erdös used to say when he found a particularly elegant prove of a theorem. He said, '*it is right out of the book*', meaning that implicitly he assumed that there is a godly book with all superior proofs of mathematical hypothesis. I am not Erdös, but I share his attitude to work on completing a never-ending puzzle.' Omega could only accept Llewellyn's confession, he liked him. He even shared a bit his fascination by the world of abstraction, though this was not enough to get a clearer picture of his own army of Blue Meanies, of the disturbances that he experienced as being unbearable. Unbearable? His life was much too convenient and his mental and physical constitution was much too strong to call something 'unbearable'. At least in the short-run, even in the mid-run, he could bear everything. There it was again: the time-horizon that had appeared in his text.

Perhaps the specification of time-horizons was a central feature necessary to identify the Blue Meanies. In the short-run the damages done to the biological environment of the human species could be ignored, to maximize capital accumulation, capital growth, could count as ultimate goal. Just like eating as much and as fast as possible appears as the optimal choice for a human individual with an extremely short time-horizon. Forget about long-run consequences like obesity or starving in winter times. But wait, Omega thought. The concept of time-horizon is always linked to an entity, to the entity that uses this time-horizon for its internal model-building. Entities at different organisational levels of the human species will probably maintain different time-horizons. An individual human being starts off with a rather short time horizon, Omega thought. The lengthening of the time horizon only comes with its subsequent embedding in its social context, e. g. by having children. This more species- oriented longer time-horizon usually is coded in a more or less explicit social contract, in moral demands, ethics, and the like. Production units, firms represented by firm owners, rely on the production cycles they are based on, on geography, seasons and manageable labour inputs. These determine their primary time-horizon. Parallel to this production cycle the flow towards the demand of the products has to be taken into consideration. In a monetary political economy with extended division of labour firm owners have to sell their products to get their profit as a sum of money. What is new in the capitalism is that this money profit frees itself from any specific form – from any particular economic sector – to be newly invested. Wherever it came from it can wander to wherever the highest expected profit rate in the shortest expected time is offered. Suddenly – in developed capitalism – the shortening of the time-horizon becomes a welcome and necessary ingredient of the internal models used by the masters of the production process. For capital not the specific production of a commodity or service plays a role, only how fast and with which profit rate the invested money returns determines where the money flows to. The short-term horizon is pivotal, mid-term and long- term-horizons only appear as sources of risk – to be hedged against: Take the money and run. It is only straight-forward that with these premises the doors for all kinds of self-destructing dynamics of advanced capitalism are wide open. Capital, articulated by its managers, is necessarily blind to any long-time perspective of the human species, it only recognizes that its accumulation process becomes riskier. Global financial crises, wars and global pandemics are getting ever more difficult to avoid. 'Here they are!', Omega all at once realized, 'These are three of the dirty dozen, which is my army of Blue Meanies.'.

Llewellyn and Omega had not spoken a word for a few minutes. Llewellyn was looking at Omega from time to time. He could see that he was in thoughts and was still waiting for a reply to his justification of a certain Platonism. But Omega's mind was elsewhere, he starred at the glass of wine on the table in front of him: 'I have to enter these thoughts in my text, and I have to tell Alpha that I now have found out about my Blue Meanies - at least approximately.'. Turning to Llewellyn he said, 'Sorry, you are right. I love you, and I feel better now.'. Llewellyn did not understand a word, but was content to be released from the silent uncertainty. They both were difficult characters – and that was what he liked about their friendship.

13 HOLD TIGHT

Alpha not only survived in her firm, she even advanced. Together with Barbarella and a newly hired junior secretary her responsibilities grew, while her work load decreased. She liked it. Venuz B. Meanie vanished, was assigned a new task at a foreign affiliate of the firm. With his disappearance many of the other Blue Meanies changed their colour, most of them to light brown. They did their jobs, but many of their jobs slowly were automated, transferred to robots. Within a few months part time work became the rule, not only in her firm but economy-wide she could see the trend. To maintain household income workers had to find more than one part-time job, a difficult task. The majority of people out in the streets became more and more nervous. Being split between different unstable jobs, between feeling better than the growing mass of pitiable migrants from the poor Global South and feeling jealousy and hate for the rich and beautiful staring from the pages of glossy magazines. Alpha understood why this light-brown nervous mass of people was struggling for orientation, for finding social identity. She even felt a bit ashamed that she personally had made it to reach a platform high enough above this sea of insecurity to forget – in the short-run – any dangers of economic hardship. At the same time the very visible enemy of a main Blue Meanie now had developed into a perilous mixture of light-brown Meanies, and it was hard to tell which of them were really mean – or good. She felt that she had to tell herself that her emotional world needed to switch from individualized relations to a positioning of herself in macro-dynamics of the whole society. But a judgement on the politically volatile nervous mass of voters, which was necessary to say something about her own position, such a judgement was something new for her. She was brought up in a political environment where established political parties – Tories and the social-democratic Left – were a fixed background. Her family, including herself, always had belonged to the Left. But at least since Toni Blair this did not mean a lot, ideological orientation was provocatively declared to be dead. She did not care.

Only now, the deeply brown Meanies within the light-brown mass of disoriented voters, the neo-fascist hardcore, started to frighten her. It became clearer with every day that their goal was to seize state power, they came nearer to it with every newly emerging crises of capitalism. The only thing they still missed to succeed was a charismatic leader, Alpha feared. She began to read the political news in mass media and social networks. The mess was frightening: On the one hand, Western mass media were politically streamlined to an extent that she never would have thought to be possible. Journalism in these fields just consisted of the rolling out of how the ruling elites, the ruling classes, interpreted what they thought to be important. On the other hand, a polarizing stream of strange speculations fighting 'the system' excelled in ignoring important empirical facts. Without the necessary theoretical background, it remained impossible to put forward a consistent alternative interpretation of what was happening. Alpha knew pretty well that she did not have this background either, but she would have liked to acquire it. In the world of social media, it could not be found.

Talking to Barbarella did not help. Barbarella was a serious user of social media, she loved it. She took part in several electronic communities, with different identities, which she was excited to invent. Sometimes as a lesbian mother of a teenager, sometimes as an elderly rich gentleman looking for an escort. Groups with explicit political content she found boring. 'It is like dreaming.', she told Alpha, 'But the difference is that you can start and end the dream whenever you want.' Alpha did not answer, only smiled mildly. 'I am afraid that the worst of these dreams might translate into a nightmare, into a sinister reality sometimes.', she thought.

In the evening, alone in her apartment, she suddenly remembered that the one thing that the Blue Meanies in Yellow Submarine hated most was *music*, in particular beat music. 'Was there any music around these days?', she asked herself. Of course, there was! But the frightening fact was that she could not tell what kind of music this was. It seemed to be *noise*. The modern light-brown Meany army had changed the strategy: Instead of forbidding music, to achieve silence it now produced massive noise and masked it as the new form of music. Wherever a little bit of music peeped around a corner to remind on what music once had been, there quickly came a monstrous tank of fully orchestrated 'improved' interpretation that stomped it into the muddy ground of deafness. When she told this observation to Omega on the phone – they used to call each other once a week – he could not stop laughing. 'You are so funny and you are perfectly right! This is why today we are forced to select what we choose to hear much more carefully. It is not so easy to find out if behind the permanent noise at some occasions a bit of music is hiding. And those of us producing these last jewels really have a hard time.', Omega was pausing, then he continued, 'I am thinking of Umberto Eco's text – I forgot the title – where he predicts that we approach a new dark age again. Monasteries are forming and are closing their walls to prevent the flood of public cultural garbage to enter their little islands. Places where they keep the treasure chests containing all the accumulated knowledge and culture of bygone days to make them available when the dark times are overcome. In that vein we can expect small and semi-secret groups of valuable musicians not going public, but keeping a selected audience in their vicinity. Pearls for the long-run.' Alpha did not know Omega's inner dialogue concerning long-run time horizons, but she liked the image of pearls. 'This not only is a nice image for the survival of music, a similar argument should hold for the creators of text. Today we are all drowned in a sea of words and sentences, most of them meaningless and useless business advertisements. Or these texts are just mirrors for the disorientation of their authors. This is one of the few areas where environmental pollution is completely ignored: informational pollution. Despite this information flood, it is almost impossible to find a text worth reading. If you enter one of the remaining better book shops, then you have to search by the name of authors, which you either know already or which have been recommended by a good friend whom you really can trust. Never rely on the judgement of the established 'literature circles' that are firmly rooted in mass media business. Maybe the use of internet communication, of electronically formed islands, of e-monasteries, is one of the good things that the IT revolution enabled.', Alpha sighed. Omega nodded, Alpha could not see it, but she felt his agreement. 'You know, I met Llewellyn.', he said, 'Llewellyn indeed is a very lonely person, I think. He lives in an abstract world, a bit like this character Jeremy Hillary Boob, the *Nowhere Man*, in Yellow Submarine – if you remember. But he is content with his life, has not discovered yet how lonely he is. Though, talking to him … I not only was forced to explain to him what progressive contradictions are, why their discovery and their exposition for the blinded mass of people is my fight against my Blue Meanies, I also felt a certain similarity to my own situation: I am longing for your company. Do you think we could meet again? Maybe in the Iron Maiden Saloon tomorrow evening?'. Alpha liked the idea. She had not exactly understood what he meant with *creative contradictions*, but the warmth of his voice in what he said afterwards convinced her. Probably the pushing each other apart needs to be ended. 'Why not? We could exchange the experiences we made in walking alone again. Ten o'clock?', she briefly regretted if this sounded too distant. It had simply been the case that focusing on one's own personality did breed some distance. Their unity survived as a memory, an extremely intense memory though. 'Okay, great!', Omega gasped. Did he really gasp, or was it only the telephone line, which distorted his voice? Alpha felt obliged to ease the situation; she started to tell him a first piece of her victory over the Blue Meanies, perhaps enriched with her conclusion to pay more attention to *grand politics*, her doubts about the usefulness of a narrow individualist perspective. Though she never had seen herself subscribing to this perspective, it might have been the case that her suspicion of others putting forward 'grand theories' – manipulation was all around and its promoters were only too visible – had hindered her too much to go beyond her very specific personal experiences. In other words, she might have mistaken her experiences too much as representative for the 'true' experiences of everybody else. But no! This second point about her doubts was too subtle to be communicated via telephone, it needed eye contact. Venuz B. Meanie's journey to hell was a story that was colourful enough to enhance the prospects for tomorrow's meeting. Of course, both of them mainly thought about having sex again. Not losing a word on this topic was part of the game.

She still was at home in her apartment, but now Alpha was happy. Omega's presence on the phone, his voice, talking to him, the expected rendezvous – all that conjured up a smile in her face. On the radio she had discovered 'Classic Pop of the 60-ties', a radio station with a mixture of songs that she had loved when she was a little girl. Now she turned it on and caught just the end of a song she always had liked a lot. She had forgotten the name of the group; it had been long and hard to remember. She looked it up in the internet: Dave Dee, Dozy, Beaky, Mick and Tich. Crazy! The song was *Hold Tight*. A perfect fit to her reapproaching Tango Wave indeed. She turned the music louder. The next song was *Satisfaction*.

Iron Maiden Saloon: Omega was there too early; it was 9.30 and he was much too excited. Brian, the barkeeper, came to his table, 'You are waiting for her?'. It was the first time that the barkeeper spoke to him, the functional talk for taking orders does not count. But Omega knew that his name was Brian. The boys having their beers at the bar sometimes called him like that. 'Yes.', he looked up, somewhat surprised. Brian had brought him the usual glass red wine, which they both always had ordered during their frequent meetings – a few weeks ago. 'She is a good girl, you should not let her go.', Brian grinned a friendly grin, which Omega would have thought to be an impossible expression for this punk face. 'Yes, she is. We are a perfect match, not just for dancing the Tango to heavy metal.'. For a moment the eyes in Brian's face flashed, then it froze again. He turned, and a minute later came back with a second glass of red wine. He put it on Omega's table without a further word.

Alpha entered the saloon 5 minutes too early. She saw the two glasses, Omega's already half empty, and looked blissfully happy. Omega was taken away; she was so beautiful. All what she had experienced had to be told to him, she immediately started to talk, to drown him in all the things she had done, she had thought. She needed him. For Omega it was good enough to look at her, to hear her voice, to participate in her adventures.

Brian, standing behind the bar, looked more often to their table than usually. He had made a bet – with himself – how long it would take until they would leave the bar, disappear in the night. Brian number one said less than 30 minutes, Brian number 2 held that it would take a little bit longer. Brian number one did win.

This night was spent in Omega's apartment. They had sex in every single room – his apartment was considerable larger than Alpha's apartment – and not just once in every room. But knowing each other's desires now better than before, they took more time, made breaks, talked a lot in between. When they finally fell asleep in Omega's bed, bodies closely entangled, it was already morning, the first sun beams creeped through the window.

Alpha did not show up in her office that day. Barbarella had an idea what must have happened. When Alpha finally called her Alpha's voice confirmed her suspicion. In a conspiratorial undertone Alpha whispered, 'For me the third sexual revolution took place last night.'. Barbarella was excited, 'Tell me more!'. 'Later. I'll be back in office tomorrow morning and we will talk after work. Today I have a light flue.', she giggled and hang up. Back at home Alpha searched 'Hold Tight', turned it loud and sang along, dancing through all rooms of her apartment.

Barbarella was somewhat embarrassed. This was not what her mantra sentence 'I am still waiting for the third sexual revolution.' was aiming for. This should be revolution on a global scale, it should initiate a long-run change. She was not jealous for Alpha's incredible night; Alpha was her best friend. And perhaps it needed this sort of singular, outstanding short-term

explosion of happiness to give hope in a slowly downgrading world. Like short-living, extremely strong candles when the darkness of an upcoming storm already obscures the contours of a possible brighter day in the future. 'Still, I wait for the third sexual revolution.', she thought melancholically.

14 WAR

'The way people in the richer countries experienced the return of global wars was first of all a fast decrease in welfare. Global value chains did not work the way customers in the North had become used to. Commodities did not arrive in the factories and shops, in the short-run substitution was rarely possible. The decrease of the global division of labour – for a long time based on well-organized exchange rate exploitation of the global working class – had its consequences: Less consumption of a decreasing variety of goods and services. The already existing status of far-reaching oligopolies in most economic branches was quickly further expanding. Only the fattest firms were able to survive by compensating their losses coming from less global division of labour by swallowing market shares from smaller competitors that faced bankruptcy. And evidently, leading wars changed the production structure of states. The weapon industries and all its surrounding branches – including scientific research in that field – flourished. The big players, the major firms in the new production system, needed a direct influence on their central customers: the war-leading states. Thus, they pushed for autocratic leaders, possible marionettes that could align a sufficient part of the state's population as supporters of his or her nationalist war. The strengthening of state power in turn had to be accompanied by a tremendous increase of manipulation by centrally controlled mass media. This sudden stream-lining of information, of mostly already globally produced information, was the second development that households in the rich North remarked – if they remarked it at all. Psychological techniques had been advancing considerable during the last decades. To use them for political warfare was not new, but much more efficient nowadays. In the successful war-supporting industries sudden price hikes, falsely blamed on war necessities, could be used to collect large amounts of extra-profits. As an immediate consequence wealth and income distribution between rich and poor parts of the population rapidly turned into horrific inequality. As in the times of the interwar period of the 20th century such a development only could fuel more and more nationalist war propaganda.'

Obviously, the discussions with an Alpha who had told him about her increasing interest in more global political economy dynamics had been transmitted to his text. His text was dictating him an explanation for Alpha's open questions. It was a lucky incidence that Omega once had studied economic theory for some years, a knowledge which the text could use. After this night of extreme sexuality Omega was not able to have his own theoretic thoughts. He was the slave of his text, which dictated him what to write next. A radical form of alienation for him that he never had experienced before. This must have been the way an Evangelist must have felt two thousand years ago. He did not like this observation; his text was in direct opposition to any religious believe in a God.

The text starred at him, then sent him to the kitchen. Omega heated water, took a cup from the cupboard, took a teabag. Waited till the water was boiling, poured it into the cup, waited again for a minute. Opened the fridge, took the milk, put milk – just two drops – into the cup. Omega took his cup and sat down at the kitchen table. He looked at the kitchen window, saw the highest branches of the tree in the backyard. The leaves did not move. No wind, it was a very hot June. The hottest June ever, as he had heard in the radio. While zipping his tea – it still was too hot - he thought, 'The long-run is turning into a short-run catastrophe'. The text had seized him again. He left the cup of tea in the kitchen and went back to the screen.

'The climate catastrophe, which now starts to occur in the short-run, mid-run at best, will add substantial drama to the dynamics of global political economy. Mass migration from some of the poorest areas in the global South will reveal how impotent so-called 'development policies' of the rich North are. In the end the northern areas sheltered by military forces in authoritarian governed border countries – the vassals of the rich centres – will just watch in TV how masses of poor people will be killed; either by natural disasters or by soldiers in the permanent wars at the borders. The disoriented mass of what once thought of itself to be the middle class of the rich North will be dividing into two polarising groups: a neo-fascist group of nationalists and a group of global humanist pacifists. Evidently this implies civil war in the North. Aggressive nationalists not only will push for wars to defend from the poor South, they will also line up against each other in the North. Internationalised war industries will try to limit the latter development to avoid disturbances of their global business. Global capitalism indeed will enter its most difficult, its most cruel stage. The collapse of global production chains, the general decrease of welfare, will make it impossible to meet the aspirations of poor countries, to enable the introduction of basic infrastructure there. Authoritarian dictators, local war heroes will be king. Whatever their rigid regimes will leave as living rest will be permanently threatened to be extinguished by the consequences of environmental deterioration. The situation will get out of control for global capital rapidly. Weapons and surveillance techniques sold to military leaders will be the ropes on which big capital will be hanged. The killing forces will themselves not be representatives of an international working class – the famous citation of Lenin on that topic, 'They will sell us the rope on which we will hang them', is a fake - but a wild mixture of more or less local war lords. It is unclear if some islands of humanity might survive this combined

collapse of environmental conditions and global capitalism.'

Omega was surprised that this doomsday scenario of his text did not leave him depressed. Quite to the contrary, he felt at ease, freed from undefined sinister hunches. To have painted these dangers on the wall of the dark cave of his existence made it easier to think about the chances to survive. A situation not too far away from the hunters in the stone age. He thought about talking about his text with Alpha, showing her what he had written so far. But this thought let the text's alarm bells ring: 'This is a very bad idea! Do not share me with the woman you love. Do not mix up your individuality with the independent processes of arguing. Forget it - immediately!', the text ordered him. Omega was not used to such a harsh tone from the text. This never had happened before. Nevertheless, he felt that he would obey. The text might leave him, if he objected, might look for another author to express itself. And perhaps Alpha would also be disgusted to find out that Omega had a second love – though a completely different kind of passionate affection was at work there. He might lose both, the text and Alpha. The text should remain his private affair, he decided. 'It takes two to Tango?', he asked himself. Or, was this a definitive statement, which the text just had uttered? Anyway, the text sighed in relieve.

Alpha and Omega met again during her lunch break. They had decided that the Iron Maiden Saloon belonged to night life, it should not exist during daytime. So, they agreed to meet in the corner of an innocent pub, not too close to her office to avoid meeting disturbing colleagues, but close enough to leave enough time for chatting. They liked the pub's name, 'The Pink Dragon'. They also agreed to have their nights, regular sex twice a week, usually at Omega's apartment. They now knew, they needed it. The approaching war times had changed Alpha. She talked a lot about what to do now, what was urgent, when they sat in the Pink Dragon. 'In wartimes men in the age between 16 and 60 are drafted, are forced by the state to become soldiers. With martial law replacing civil law a strictly hierarchical order system is implemented. You will not be allowed to use your own thoughts to choose your actions, you will be forced to do what your commander orders you, Omega.', she said. 'The Omega I know,

the man I love, will be dead, will have been turned into a tool of a mostly anonymous state power. Even before he comes into the danger of being killed in a battle.', her soft voice was in stark contrast to the panic, which the content of her words transported. 'This is the truth about war. We have to organise, build resistance groups, find ways to survive in an environment that will be more and more a police state with IT-surveillance everywhere. CCTV was only the starting shot here in England. Maybe, we should start with an innocent, very small network of people keeping up communication, four or five persons. Communication beyond the garbage that the mass media are feeding to the zombies that they train for the wars of their masters. Maybe, I ask Barbarella and you ask Llewellyn to participate in our group; perhaps the younger girl, Lucy, that supports Barbarella now in the office, would be a possible fifth member of our cell.', Alpha's eyes were asking Omega for an answer. 'I like the word 'cell'.', he quickly said, 'And I think this is a brilliant idea. Tell me a bit more about Lucy. Any vibrant cell has to consist of a diversity of its smaller entities, which contributes not only to its flexibility, but also keeps its internal communication lines swinging. Good vibes, good music, is the stuff that helps to keep internal unity alive.', now Omega smiled. 'At the edge of war, we will persist – we even will thrive.', he could not help to add this last pathetic sentence. 'Sorry', he thought. Alpha was glad that Omega liked her ideas.

She did not know much about Lucy, only what Barbarella had been telling her. Barbarella now often spent her lunch break with Lucy while Alpha was meeting Omega. In the following week Alpha arranged to have a common dinner of Barbarella, Lucy and herself. It turned out to be a game changing event. At least at the office they now where a tightly knit little group. When Alpha met Omega in the 'Pink Dragon' again, she told him Lucy's story.

.

15 GENERATION Z

Lucy was a wizard; she always had been. As a young school girl teachers loved her. She was quick, vivid and understood arguments almost instantaneously. Her parents were both teachers, biology and mathematics, before they decided to leave Poland in the early 90-ties to migrate to England. Lucy was born when they already lived in the suburbs of London. When she was fifteen Lucy started to change. She started to experience more and more consciously that she was a migrant, was non-British. Her boyfriend John was a nice guy, but he once explained, 'I am a white boy, a Londoner, you are also white - though a migrant girl. I don't mind, but there always will be some difference between us.'. After that she could not consider him as a friend any more. 'But he is correct.', she had to admit. The groups of close friends really started to separate in her teenage years. Then her father lost his job, luckily her mother continued to being employed. The tightening financial situation made it clear that she would not get a chance to attend a higher education institution. With seventeen she started to look for a job to contribute to the family income. Even when, after a year, her father started to work as a taxi driver, the plan to finance a better education for Lucy was out of consideration. She found a first part-time job as clerk in a wholesale company.

It was a bit frustrating for the clever young girl with the vivid intellect. And it left her a considerable amount of time to look for more challenging opportunities. Fortunately, there was aunt Molly. She was not a real aunt, not the sister of one of her parents, she only was an old friend of her mother since their common days in Poland. And Molly was only the nickname that everyone in London used, her original first name was Malgorzata. Though she liked this name, she quickly turned it to 'Molly' when she arrived in London. People should remember her name easily. Aunt Molly was a real intellectual. She had made her PhD in Warsaw and then, in London, was accepted as a librarian in one of the university libraries. Contrary to this gratifying success her marriage with her husband did not go well. Lucy only knew aunt Molly as a divorced woman, the husband had returned to Poland. Lucy used to visit aunt Molly several times a week, Molly even took Lucy to her office, letting her read selected books in the outer office before having lunch or dinner together. It was quite idyllic. The groups of same-age boys and girls of the migrant community hardly interested Lucy. She started to live in the richer world promised in the books she read. These were not randomly chosen books. Aunt Molly was an upright socialist since her youth. As such she had hated the Stalinist police regime of the Polish government before the revolt of Lech Wałęsa's Solidarnośc. But when Wałęsa's movement rapidly became a close ally of the catholic church, Malgorzata – the convinced atheist - decided that Polish politics were disgusting. Together with her husband, a technical engineer, they migrated to England. Aunt Molly loved the civilized manners of the British. She was active in the socialist party of the country, but even in that role her hate for the Tories always was garnished with a breeze of respect. Aunt Molly saw it as her most important privilege to offer her fine-tuned attitudes and styles to her would-be daughter Lucy. Maybe she would develop similar preferences.

And indeed; Lucy soon developed her own requisite taste. The books by certain Marxist historians and economists were paralleled by a penchant for cynics like Oscar Wilde. Even scientific outcasts like Nicolai Tesla could incite her attention. Her close relationship with Aunt Molly made Lucy an attentive observer of British politics too. They both were infuriated by the consequences of Tony Blair's turn to what he called 'New Labour'. Supporting the US President Bush in his attack on Iraq had disqualified Blair as a leader of a labour party in a European country. During the internal chaos in the British labour party that followed its defeat in the next elections Molly distanced herself more and more from this party. She now had to rely on her own judgements concerning the dynamics of political economy even more than before. The official, publicly presented party lines were of no help, even the spurious traces of a consistent strategy were disappearing. In her search for explanations the discussions with Lucy became ever more helpful. The young girl looked at the connections between upcoming events with a fresh mind. She saw underlying networks of causality earlier and clearer than Molly. Aunt Molly often pressed emerging relationships in the Procrustean bed of left-right politics too quickly, ignoring important details. And Lucy learned to argue, Molly still was a tough defender of her view.

While Lucy had never been exposed to professional academic life – perhaps because she had missed the purely academic play of critique and counter-critique – she developed into a highly intellectual young girl. The alienation from same-age migrant circles was a straight forward consequence. Her aunt Molly was the anchor around which her vivid mind was floating – meeting other influences mainly in the books she read. Her life had entered a new stage. Her parents considered themselves as a-political, they rapidly stopped any debate that Lucy tried to initiate – friendly, but decisively. They had left a country which had been torn apart by politics, a country that now did fall back in the worst type of nationalism. They simply were fed-up with politics; they now preferred the polite business-minded British population. They were predictable and cool – somehow. No great ideas, no pathos, but with pitiless British humor. Too bad that they had to struggle hard to pay their bills, but they survived and their daughter will have a good life. 'To be honest', Lucy thought, 'they love me more than I love them.'.

The one thing that Lucy always had in the back of her mind was her fascination with music. Even while reading she used to have her earphones on, listening to some of her favorite jazz tunes. Jazz was her thing. It was old, but not too old. The roots, as far as she knew, somewhere in the interwar period. And then so many meanders till today, each one exciting and surprising. The musicians involved in this flow were like rocks changing the directions of this river of jazz, giving it new impetus. In the end these rocks were not interesting for her. She was not an archivist of jazz history. Single jazz musicians were lonely towers only, lonely as she was. But they kept the flow going. Sometimes she wondered how this direct connection from jazz music to her mind, to her mood, worked. But this remained to be only a sudden glimpse of a thought. 'It works; don't ruin it by analysing it.', she stopped herself. She didn't like classic music as she didn't like almost all variants of modern pop music. Only some of the lyrics that she inevitably snaped up did stick to her memory. One could use them if they characterised a situation particularly well. Lucy never had to learn an instrument. Her mother had learned to play piano in Poland, but in London there was no room for such an instrument – and no money. In class, as a pupil, several boys practised to play guitar and two female class mates were sure they will become famous singers. Bands emerged and faded away within months. Nobody was interested in her favorite instrument, the saxophone, or in jazz music in general. She stayed lonely.

One evening, out of the blue, Lucy decided to go out. To frustrate potential boyfriends, which repeatedly were asking her, had become her standard behaviour. She had convinced herself that somebody who was inviting her to go out never could be as interesting as somebody she would have chosen as an adequate partner. It was the trap of lonely girls, she knew it. And then, all of a sudden, her wish to go out was there and she saw no reason why not following this wish. Her parents were not surprised at all; they had been already wondering why a pretty young girl like her daughter always stayed at home in the evening. Of course, she did not know where to go, so she decided to do the evident: Lucy went to Soho and dived into the first club she found to be adequately filled up

with young people. It was there, where she met Barbarella.
The first thing that Lucy noticed when she entered was the noise, and as part of the noise what should have been music. She was appalled. All she could detect was simple repetition of the beat of a synthetic drum. But then she saw the many smiling faces talking, or rather shouting at each other and she remembered that this was her plan: Go out, let yourself fall into something completely new, completely different, don't care, dare it! The first best thing to do in this strange environment was to dance. Or better: to move your body with the frequency of the stomping rhythm machine. This was not music, no jazz; but she was alone and was out to experience a new world. She had assured herself in advance that it was mandatory not to have any expectations. The essence of something new was that it had to be absolutely free from any prejudices. She started moving, first only with her legs, then a little dangling with her arms, in between she closed her eyes for a few seconds. She started to get used to it, almost liked it. Suddenly somebody spoke to her, 'Hey you', a girl's voice, 'you are new here, I never saw you before.'. Lucy turned her head to the voice. 'Yes, I'm here for the first time. Nice place.', she lied. 'I don't really like it.', the other girl replied, 'I could show you a much nicer place, if you want.'. Lucy instinctively realised that this other girl was also a single. Not in the sense of several other seemingly single girls in the room, hanging around with a bunch of boys each of whom they knew pretty well – girls on the transition line between boys; no, this other girl was as single as Lucy was. They both went together to a neighbouring location, something half café, half bar. 'My name is Barbarella. Funny, no?', the other girl said. 'My name is Lucy.', a short reply, a second of silence. She wants to tell me the story of her naming, Lucy thought. But she was wrong. Barbarella said, 'Like 'Lucy in the Sky with Diamonds'?'. Barbarella smiled. Lucy did not know what to do with this sentence. She might have been only two or three years younger than Barbarella but she had never heard of the famous Beatles song. 'Your parents must have adored LSD when they chose your name. I like it. Your name, not LSD. I never took drugs, some alcohol, of course.'. They both had a glass of wine.

After a few more common evenings, Lucy found the new evening entertainment increasingly pleasant, the two girls knew almost everything about each other. Lucy had heard Barbarella's steady mantra dozens of times already: 'I am still waiting for the third sexual revolution.'. And it was Lucy who explained to Barbarella its deeper historical context, or what Lucy thought this context could be. Barbarella loved to listen to her, though with one eye she was sometimes at the bar, at the single men hanging around there. Just like showing me what the content of her steady sentence was about. The music in this new place in general was bearable, Lucy found.

When the new boss in Barbarella's firm announced that business had been extended and Alpha should get more agenda a new clerk, Barbarella immediately talked to Alpha: 'I know the best choice for this job. Her name is Lucy, she's a good friend and a very intelligent person.'. Alpha always had been a team-oriented executive. The wisdom of management courses that praised competition and separation between employees to increase productivity was complete rubbish in her eyes. Jealousy kills, not only in private life but also in business environments. Lucy got the job, Alpha's instincts one more time proved to be correct. Two weeks later the three women met in the darkest corner of a nearby cafeteria. After two hours of exchanging stories about her personal lives, Alpha proposed an agreement on how to handle their professional cooperation: The side constraint to be observed was that Alpha could present to her boss an achievement of her team, which was satisficing, that means 'no complaints'. In regarding this constraint each of the three should minimize her work-time input, of course, without hurting the efforts of the other two colleagues. A sufficiently high level of trust should be enabled by weekly meetings outside the firm, which should secure that in emergency cases work-time inputs could be substituted by helping team-members – even without any time-schedule monitoring. An important additional agreement was that all in-group communication should remain within the team. They would be an independent cell within the larger framework of the firm. The interface between the firm and their cell should be managed exclusively by Alpha, which implied an extra portion of trust on her. Barbarella and Lucy empathetically agreed on this amendment. As long as the financial survival of the firm was ensured the survival of the finances of the three team members should be secured too. After three intense hours the pact of the cell was celebrated.

When Lucy met Molly the next day, Molly immediately noted that her younger companion emanated an air of confidence and joy. She told her and Lucy nodded; but she did not tell her the reason for her perfect mood. She now was part of an independent cell. Secretly Lucy thought that she should have a look at organic cell formation. To know more about this topic on a more abstract, theoretical level should be fun. At home she would look it up in google and make some notes. This was generation-Z Lucy, the other side of generation-Z Barbarella.

16 STRATEGY CALLING

Omega came home with the feeling that his text urgently needed him. The war now was coming really close. Official statements of several leaders in European states openly were calling to reduce expenditures for public welfare to have enough money for weapons and the equipment of soldiers. It was clear that well-paid professional killer groups would not suffice to lead a full-scale war, parts of the domestic population would have to be drafted. The emancipation of women implied that there also would be many female soldiers drawn to war, particularly in Britain. Alpha came into his mind.

Alpha's ideas had impressed Omega. She was right and he would support any effort she would make. She was not only a lover; on a more general level, she also was a comrade. Building a cell with a small group of diverse members was an excellent idea. The raison d'être of such a cell was communication, to elaborate, to interpret what was going on in the world. This task was a healthy ingredient for the evolution of each member's self-understanding, it enabled an existence as part of a larger social entity. For the internal communication process, the outer borderline of the cell was important since otherwise the permanent public noise produced to silence cells, to hinder their emergence, would distort all interpretations. A minimum of internal clarity was a precondition for any action of a conscious social entity. But what was an 'action'? To be self-sustaining, to satisfy the cell's members seemed to be not enough to qualify for the concept of 'action'. All that was only a preliminary condition to act as a cell. It was a kind of short-run tactic ensuring that the cell was not destroyed. Omega had read the classic book 'On War' by Clausewitz and thus knew how to distinguish between tactic and strategy. So far, their cell would only work on incoming information and use it to maintain its member's - and its own - survival. This was the necessary short-run tactic of survival. What they needed, in the long run, was outgoing action; action eventually including outgoing information. To shape actions, to find out what they might be, it needed a strategy. Clausewitz in his time had a very specific goal, namely to win a war that consisted of a sequence of shorter-run battles. What should his cell's goal be, was its survival in the all-surrounding wars enough? Definitely not, Omega thought. And with this thought, he felt that his text was calling. It cried, 'Keep on writing, I might show you some hints on strategy!'. Omega followed this order, opened his laptop, read the last paragraphs of the text, and started writing.

'The trouble with definitive doomsday predictions is that they leave the reader not only speechless, they also are mute concerning actions. The world is caught in its inevitable dynamics. To revive the perspective of actions it is necessary to take a closer look at these dynamics. Look at the new political dictators and their seeming omnipotence. For the handling of confused masses, it has proved useful to have a single person, a charismatic leader, in the communication sphere maintained by mass media. With a little bit deeper inspection, it can be seen that this leader always is a marionette, an actor put up by a larger group, a group steering a military-industrial complex. The disintegrating capitalism of the 21st century has been falling apart in three large parts, each one with a specific military-industrial complex: the US, China and Russia. Local wars along the borders of these three empires should not deceive an observer that the underlying industrial relations between the three pseudo-imperial superstructures are pretty tight – they are interdependent. Not only the financial network linking China to the USA is considerably more developed than most journalistic commentators and war propagators would have it, despite noisy rhetoric there also is a tight relationship between military circles in Russia and the USA. Without permanent limited attack and 'necessary' retaliation the importance of the military, the need to reduce general social welfare to finance it, could be called into question. It takes two to Tango.'

Omega stopped. What was this sentence in this context? Never mind; and he continued writing.

'If the industrial aspect and the military aspect disentangle somewhat this means that two scenarios are possible: Either a dominant military leadership on all three sides achieves a continuing flow of waves of limited wars supported by a continuing decrease of welfare of all populations. Or a dominance of industrial leadership can overcome military influences and a kind of truly global disintegrating capitalism emerges. This would not be big fun either, of course. World-wide, IT-supported surveillance techniques – partially supported by tailored police and military force – will lead to unprecedented levels of global exploitation of humans by humans. Will new IT-technologies allow the exploiters to be able to hide their exploitation activities from the exploited? And, how all this fits to deteriorating environmental conditions always will stay an additional question. Where are the cracks in these downward spirals that could enable social

subjects to induce a counter movement? Hundred eighty years ago Karl Marx visited the factory floors of the firm of his friend Friedrich Engels and saw there the workers, saw the proletariat. As a good Hegelian he immediately concluded that progress proceeds by a fight – and a victory - of the most contradictory element to the status quo, which then in turn will enable a qualitatively new level of state of affairs. Thus, he identified the proletariat as the motor of progress. Hegel's three methodological steps – thesis, antithesis, synthesis - did only allow two antagonistic forces, which breed the new element synthesis. So, Marx thought that the historical record was showing that all formerly existing classes would melt down to two opposing classes: the capitalist class and the working class. As Marx himself tended to admit the developments after the failed revolution of 1848 showed that this assumption was wrong. He died before he would have seen how nationalist ideologies would tear apart German and French working classes during World War 1, not to speak about 20th century's Fascism, that turned his gloomy analysis of anti-Semitism written in 1843 into the cruelest reality carried out by a new type of movement. This movement was not a class in the economic sense that Marx had attached to the concept of class, the clue that held – and still holds - fascists together was a strange brew of ideologically twisted contradictions. Still, even today and in particular globally, the divide into the two classic economic classes of exploiters and exploited can be calculated. But in the 21st century the force of ideology-based movements has become overwhelming. Religions, fascist and nationalist political parties, and the like are flourishing. Each movement that passes a lower threshold of force attracts financial investors instrumentalizing it.'

Omega had to take a deep breath. The text continued:

'Coming back to the two possible scenarios, military-led and industry-led: Where are the cracks in their respective dynamics? They have to be found at places where authoritarian capitalism will fail to solve a contradiction, which it repeatedly produces. Ever more catastrophic environmental conditions, deteriorating income and wealth inequalities are typical examples. In a military-led world a weakening economic production system would imply that more direct, coercive exploitation will occur. A renaissance of the slavery mode of production – warrior hierarchies exploiting their slaves – though with modern technology can be expected. A breaking of such a regime might only be expected if the rivalries and wars between empires weakens all of them sufficiently to allow for a revolution of the slaves. Until this point, if it ever occurs, the 'monasteries' have to survive in the dark. If on the other hand the industry-led scenario succeeds, then chances for earlier cracks in the dynamics of an overexpanding reign of the capitalist algorithm might be somewhat better. Oligopolisation in most branches has proceeded far enough to advance to the jump from private global monopoly to global public ownership. In particular the dire state of affairs apparent through the climate catastrophe produced by monopolists makes the need of democratically organised public institutions visible for everybody. To develop democratic mechanisms is not a trivial task, as in particular the example of the emergence of a global knowledge base – Wikipedia? – shows.

Who might be the social force that can widen the cracks that appear in the policies of private oligopolies and monopolies, can fill them with democratic content that breaks their private character? In biology a common myth had been that it is always the bigger and stronger species, which sets an end to a disappearing species. Scientific consideration showed that this rarely was the case. It usually was an invasion of a large number of smaller intruding living species, which initiated the fall, or the basic change, of a species. Therefore, it might be speculated that – contrary to the 19th century belief in the strong unit of an international proletariat – it indeed might be an increasing mass of small and diverse progressive cells spread all across the world, which ring in the end of authoritarian global capitalism. Even the already mentioned difficulty to replace the short-sighted capitalist algorithm by long-run oriented democratic mechanisms often could be better approached by intelligent smaller progressive cells. So, after their tactical retreat necessary to survive in a hostile environment, these cells will continue their strategic goal to develop their knowledge on how to govern the world. To develop global democracy.'

Wow! Omega looked at the text. 'You are much too aspiring, much too speculative!', he wanted to tell his text. But the text did not have ears and eyes, it never listened, it only could pour out arguments. 'At least it clearly implied that progressive cells should support anti- militarism to get a chance to enter the cracks in global private monopoly capital.', he had to admit. That was a first strategic hint to work with.

The next day Omega met Alpha in the Pink Dragon. He still did not show her his text, but he told her stories about tactics and strategies and how they are to be connected. Alpha was a bit bored. She did not want to frustrate him too much, but of course all kinds of management literature, of articles on the superiority of female leadership in handling tactics and strategy, of simple rule sets for the education of small children, and the like – all that covered pretty well what Omega tried to explain to her. But okay, strategic considerations will become important for their circle, they will have to go beyond their self-sustaining interpretation meetings. While agreeing on that, Alpha was thinking of a more practical question: Where should the circle meet? She loved her partitioning of locations: Her office with the two girlfriends, her apartment as the place to rest and to recreate, Omega's apartment – or the park bench – for intense sex, the Pink Dragon for intellectual intercourse with Omega. A location that would be suitable for the meetings of their circle evidently had to be a different place. But where? Omega proposed to think about an electronic meeting place. This could make it easier for the members to attend meetings; to move your body to a geographically defined location always is a drag. And mobility in a large city like London is getting more cumbersome each year. Alpha's instincts were immediately against this proposal. First, communication via electronic media was the most monitored type of communication. Despite all the gossip about data security and safe passwords everything that exists somewhere in electronic form can be read by specialized police, military and even expert private enterprises.

The only safeguard to remain hidden is the sheer mass of monitored exchanges. To identify what is relevant for the goal at hand is extremely time consuming. This is why so much money is put to AI research; to automatise state control, to make total electronic surveillance efficient. An electronic meeting place is just another open directory in an enormous library supervised by the global network of secret services.

‘But we will not be a circle of suicide bombers or dangerous terrorists’, Omega smiled. Alpha felt that she should proceed to her second reason, ‘Additionally, I am convinced that being physically close to each other has a different quality. Location is a concept referring to a point in space, and remember physics. Each entity, each point with mass, is attracted in space by other entities proportional to the inverse square of the distance between them. It’s gravitation stupid. Even to us humans - latest fruit of physical evolution - to be close to each other counts. And as mankind recently has found out, it is gravitation that under extreme circumstances warps space-time. It might even produce space and time.’. Now Omega was stupefied, ‘You are following the debates in quantum theory? I first thought you were pointing at sexual, physical closeness – another convincing topic for me.’. ‘I did.’, now Alpha’s eyes had a certain glow, ‘Or was it rather the song on the time warp in the Rocky Horror Picture Show? Yes, I do have my hobbies.’. Omega loved her, ‘You better don’t tell Llewellyn that quantum theory is a hobby. He knows a lot about it. But seriously: I think that we have to find a special solution to our location problem. It cannot be only a compromise between our two preferences. It has to be a new combination.’. Omega was tempted to tell her more about Schumpeter, but he anticipated that this would be boring for her. She knew already that he had read a lot of old stuff. And not just funny entertainment like her black and white movies of the fifties.

The choice of a location for their future circle meetings remained an open issue on this early afternoon in the Pink Dragon. The question was looming in the back of their two brains, waiting for a moment when a new combination suddenly could leave this cerebral backyard.

17 THE PINK DRAGON

A dragon is associated with China, or with a European knight and his lance in the Middle Ages near a quagmire. The colour pink is associated with the clothes of little girls, or certain cream desserts that are much too sweet. The contrast between the two chains of associations is the creative contradiction on which the owner of the pub intended to thrive, intended to fix a place for this new combination in the brains of potential customers. He succeeded; the pub had its regulars. The name of the owner was Henry. At some occasions he used to introduce himself by 'I am the friendly Henry', and laughed when a guest said, 'Nice to meet you, friendly Hendly – oh, sorry, friendry Hendry, or so …'. All the jokes in the world were on purpose.

When Alpha and Omega had chosen the Pink Dragon as their semi-secret rendezvous location, they thought that the name is funny, that was all. Henry's trick had been working. Once Omega had been half an hour too early and Henry invited him to sit down on his table, where he was having his lunch. This was when Omega learned about the conscious choice of the name of the pub. Henry was of the opinion that creative craziness was at the heart of true entrepreneurship. Omega nodded, he thought that her choice of a location was exactly such a task demanding a crazy innovation. But he remained silent, Henry was an entrepreneur, not him. To chat a bit could be pleasant, even stimulating, but he had to keep a certain distance. Distance again, the metric of relationships, friends as locations. But these friends not only are in different distances, they also have different momentum – mass times velocity. This feeds back on the location of meeting points. What does Heisenberg's statement that it is impossible to find out location and velocity simultaneously mean in this context? Where Alpha and he a very small swinging object, like an electron. A kind of probabilistic Tango wave – whatever that should mean? Henry had been continuing to tell stories, not noticing that Omega had retired into his own thoughts. 'I have to meet my friend now, sorry.', Omega interrupted somewhat impolite Henry's stories. He pointed at Alpha who was just entering the pub, but in fact he thought about meeting Llewellyn later in the afternoon to discuss with him the isomorphisms of theoretical physics and political economy. Henry smiled and felt guilty of talking too much. After a welcome kiss Alpha and Omega went to their table in the corner of the pub.

'Somehow we should combine the advantages of the different solutions to the location problem.', Alpha started the arguments. 'Isn't it possible to escape from the retrievable part of the internet, to vanish in the mist of uncountable probabilities of uncountable items. I know that the world is always finite, but finding out a location can take more time than the expected existence of our solar system; and this would be a sufficient finiteness for us. I remember that security systems in banks work with multiplication of very large prime numbers to bring the extremely high duration time of solution algorithms into play. If a weather forecast for tomorrow needs a week to come up with a result, then tomorrow's weather will always be a speculation.'. Omega laughed, a controlled, rather polite laugh. He knew exactly what she was talking about. 'I agree. Our location has to be a moving target. A target that moves much faster than the eye of our observers is able to follow. And the places where the results of our meetings materialize, where they carry fruits, these places have to be different from the locations of our meetings. Most practical applications of AI today are stuck, since they rely on supervised learning based on pattern recognition in large data sets of empirical observations. Usually, some kind of implicit linearity assumption also plays a key role – and still it takes them a long time to come up with probable solutions. So, time can be a key element. But what about us, about the closeness of our bodies that we need? We are permanently identified and located, not just by the smartphones we carry, but also by the face recognition performed with the videos from CCTV in all public places.' Alpha was leaning back, 'I need a drink.'. With an Aperol Spritz in front of her she continued, 'In today's big cities millions of individuals roll around in rather predictable ways. Their waves – and even the average small deviations from these waves – are so regular, it is deceiving. It must be frustrating to see this if you believe in free will. But once you have estimated the small standard deviations around their trajectories you do not really know what happens during these deviations. They are small, but they are many. And what is always the trick of standard probability: It only shifts the fact of non-knowledge of content to the knowledge of the outer appearance of this non-knowledge. So, these might be the many small places where our monasteries could hide their content. If you know what I mean?'. Omega had a faint prevision of what she meant. But first of all, he again was surprised by her profound and broad knowledge. He told her. 'I do have many hobbies.', she smiled and grasped his hand across the little table. 'Tonight?', her voice was very low.

Two days later Omega met Llewellyn. He explained their plan to establish a progressive interpretation circle. Llewellyn liked it very much. 'As a starter, help us think about the location for our meetings.', he continued and gave him a short summary of what he had discussed with Alpha. 'So, it is about hiding within a deterministic chaos?', he said. 'No, not really.', he continued and corrected himself, 'Deterministic chaos only is a property of certain deterministic systems, which makes their long-run state of affairs indistinguishable from pure white noise. This is not handy enough for our purpose. What we need is something different. Have you heard about Steven Wolfram, the prodigy?'. Certainly, I knew him: 'Yes, I sometimes use his software 'Mathematica'. He is a legend.'. Lewellyn admired him too, 'He has reconstructed most of mathematics with his algorithmic new language. And not just that tiny task; with his rule 30 he produces the typical maze of pure randomness. Not distinguishable from the basic randomness taking place at smallest scales of theoretical physics, in quantum theory. We should look at that in more detail.'. Omega was content. This certainly was a good topic for one of their first meetings, quantum theory was a hobby of Alpha too. But first they had to organise a meeting, find out what they meant by 'a meeting'. Omega was scared. The exchange with Llewellyn had only led deeper into the jungle of confusion.

At home in his apartment, he stood in front of his window and thought about weather forecasts. Why was making a forecast so time consuming? It was evident that a forecast always remained a forecast because it had to make several restrictive assumptions, it only could get close to what the weather itself did. The forecast was a model, which means that it consisted of two basic elements: (1) A set of quantitative measurements at time zero in a set of qualitatively chosen essential variables, and (2) a set of rules that explicitly described how the first set changes as time proceeds. For global weather forecasts the restriction in the first element consisted in choosing a limited set of points around the world for reporting their weather conditions; plus, the choice of essential variables to be quantitatively reported. How fast measurement and transfer of the data to the centre where the model was computed could be might also play a role. The second element, the choice of appropriate algorithms to describe change over time in weather conditions at each of the selected measurement points, could be approximated rather neatly by the formulas available from physics, though with computing time exploding as the number of measured points and their variables increases. An additional difficulty for the algorithms occurs due to the emergence of new essential variables and new essential relationships in the course of time. Variables that were thought to be essential at time zero may lose their importance, while others at a later time have to be discovered by the algorithms as from now on essential ones. The same is true for the algorithms themselves! Therefore, it is not surprising that global weather still outpaces the best man-made forecasts.

At that point it dawned to Omega that locality plays an important role again: Local weather forecasts can be much better than global ones. In a smaller area the observation points can be denser, data transfer is faster and one can draw on the long-run experiences of the local population. In political economy this thought translates into a better predictability of the evolution of smaller cultural units, at least in the short-run. But the molecules of weather forecasts only communicate via basic physical laws, while human societies sometimes follow

weird waves produced by class struggle and technology. It is dangerous to be seduced by too far-reaching analogies. And then Omega remembered that he always had been asking himself why Karl Marx never had produced a concise long-run forecast on how a communist society would work. He had insisted on a critique of the prevailing capitalist society and at best provided some immediate short-run measures – after a revolution. No long-run forecast, no utopia. Marx must have sensed the dangers of long-run forecasting, probably also due to his study of his forerunners, the french utopian socialists. Their short-run tactics to survive as a small cell in interpreting and criticizing the status quo seemed to be in line with Marx scepticism. This was their stage one, a strategy for stage two could only develop slowly, right now it would be premature. For a moment he remembered the Small Red Book of Mao Tse Tung and the strategies for Guerrilla warfare: If the enemy advances – retreat, if the enemy stops – disturb him, if the enemy pulls back – follow him. The current situation, stage one, probably approached a transition from advancing to stopping of the enemy. So, it was wise to retreat and disturb a little. The choice of locality was urgent, but not too hot. He felt that the text was calling him, he turned to his desk and opened the laptop.

Meanwhile Alpha had turned her little team into a very successful and respected unit of the firm. She really started to like her work life, in particular as a contrast to what happened in geopolitics and how she expected to act politically as part of their planned circle – not to speak about the contrast to her secret sex life. Of course, what they were doing in the insurance business was a very tiny bit of the global production system, the system governed by the capitalist algorithm: act to maximize short-run profits by taking into account risks. More technically this meant that the combination of the expected mean profit expectations and the expectations of the variance of these expectations had to be optimized. It would have been a rather trivial mathematical procedure if only the involved expectation processes would have been trivial. Expectation formation was the link to the real world of political economic dynamics. At the root of the insurance business was its ability to convince potential customers that the risks they will face in the future will be higher than they currently expect. They offer a contract to take over part of the risk for a periodic payment of the customer. If the original expectation of the customer turns out to have been correct, then the insurance firm makes a profit, if not it might be confronted with a loss – it is a bet on what will happen. For Alpha it was just a mirror image of what happened in national lotteries. In that business the organizer has to twist the expectation of the customers concerning their self-evaluation of being a luckier individual than the rest. In both fields fooling the customers was the essential trick. Alpha was talking to Barbarella and Lucy about these ideas. 'Nothing is in our genes.', said Barbarella and laughed, 'We are made cautious and frightened to make us buy insurance, and the resulting gap between the insured - but bored - individual and its desire to be something special is filled with a cheap lottery ticket. We are in between the waves of paying insurance and paying for lottery tickets. But somehow people like it to be repeatedly frustrated. It is good enough for them to see selected lucky winners and selected happily insured losers on their TV screens. It provides colour to their lives.'. Lucy was less sanguine. She had just used three hours of her leisure time last night to take a look at a book, which Molly had brought her from the library: Hilferding's 'Finance Capital'. Molly had tried to raise her interest in the book by telling her that the author had intended to add a new volume to Marx epochal three volumes of 'Capital'; writing 25 years after Marx' death. The dominant role of finance in the capitalist algorithm had just become apparent at that time. Lucy's curiosity for everything concerning the history of political economy made her stay up late last night. In the interwar period the possibilities of big finance had enabled capital to float completely free between different profit opportunities – in particular in the USA, where oligopolisation moved to the fast track. Hilferding had anticipated that. The leading decision makers for these capital flows had to base their expectations on predictions of the actions of leading policy makers – and vice versa. Networks of self-sustaining expectations are rapidly fragile as soon as they lose their ground in hard economic facts: The Great Depression was a prime experience. In the USA president F.D. Roosevelt made a desperate attempt to break the power of the bosses of big industry, proposing a 'New Deal'. In Germany the old, just defeated military elite was confronted with a new political force: the fascists. The new combined ruling class – old military elite, re-emerging economic heavy weights, and the radical political innovation of racist nationalism that held them together – was constructing its new empire with breath-taking speed. Fascist ideology swept over to other parts of the world, fascist cells established themselves and survive till today. The majority of politicians outside Germany and Italy did not understand what was going on until the Nazis started WW2. All these thoughts were not explicitly materializing in Lucy's brain, of course. They were like a five second flash light of remembrance of yesterday's reading. What now, after six seconds, did strike her was the dominance of stream-lined expectations that clearly was a parallel to what happened in most present settings. 'It is so easy nowadays to fool thousands and millions of people if you have the power to control modern mass-media.', Lucy said a bit excited. 'This is not only good money for certain economic branches and the source of pollution of our information environment with ads, it is also the chance for a renaissance of fascism on a new technological level.'. 'So true!', Alpha was surprised by the strong statement of the young girl. 'Truth?', Lucy smiled mischievously, 'The only truth are the lines played by Miles Davies. Music only appears in the moment when it is played and, in this moment, can resemble truth. I don't believe in recorded truth.'. Barbarella looked surprised, 'Miles Davies, you said. Is he still alive?'.

Omega's room; his text dictating his fingers what to write. The fingers were badly trained in typing, but that did not matter much, because his thoughts evolved even slower.

'Lay back and consider your current situation. Are you fine? Is the global production system enabling you a living-standard – eating, drinking, a warm apartment in winter time, and the like – that feels good? It is the advanced global division of labour - between continents and countries, between more educated and less educated labour efforts needed – that makes this living standard possible. Despite the capitalist algorithm, which has produced this state of affairs. Has produced it at the price of enraging exploitation, omnipresent alienation and following Infantilization. The need for the capitalist algorithm now is over, in the last decades it is resulting in much more severe damages than benefits. But do living-standards, do the fruits of global division of labour have to vanish with the capitalist algorithm? Certainly not, though the mix of consumed goods and services surely will have to change. The fun of a new smartphone every year will have to be substituted by the fun of discovering a new knowledge area or a new type of cultural enjoyment every year. Maybe not every year, maybe every second year. Preserving the valuable is as important as destroying the outdated evil.
Therefore, it is of utmost importance to develop a progressive interpretation of current mechanisms. Only a careful inspection reveals what is evil and what should be preserved – though usually in an adapted form. In certain locations a well-specified market mechanism can be employed to detect preferences of a group of consumers, this is not the same as the all- embracing ideology of a 'market economy'. A deep cut will have to be made with respect to investment decisions. Since large, long-term investment always binds resources, implies missing investment somewhere else, social institutions with scientifically supported expectation formation have to be installed, often have to be invented, which substitute the short-term oriented intuition of today's private investors. Similar social innovations will pave

the way towards the next - political - global revolutionary wave and will continue for some time after its zenith.'

The text had glowing eyes. No! A text does not have eyes, Omega told himself. But it now certainly had a less dystopian air. It supported their idea to form a progressive cell with a stage one centered on survival and interpreting of current events.
When he met Alpha a few days later he proposed to choose something simple as a meeting point for their circle. He knew that there were two storage rooms of

the Pink Dragon, connected by a door behind the bar. Alpha and Omega asked Henry if he needed both of them, they would like to rent one of them as a regular, weekly meeting place for their discussion group. This second storage room could be entered from the first one, but also from a second door that led to the corridor of the neighbouring house. A friend of Henry lived there, so they would have access to corridor and storage room from the neighbouring house without disturbing bar business. It looked great, Henry saw their smiling faces and used their excitement to bargain for a rather exaggerated price. They agreed, it was an opportunity too good not to be taken. On their way home to Omega's apartment, they decided that to give their meeting point a rather common name, a name that hundreds of locations in England would share. This was the minimum-security measure they chose. They only would use this name internally. They called it 'Henry's Hideaway'.

18 SESSION DELTA

The night was falling in the streets of London, none of the persons sitting in *Henry's Hideaway* saw it. The room had two doors but no window. It had been a storage room. Omega had bought a large table and six chairs on which they now were sitting. In the corner, beside the door, there was a fridge and another little desk with a coffee machine. An old laptop stood also on this desk, in case … Alpha, Omega, Llewellin and Lucy had their own laptops on the table anyway. Barbarella liked to be spontaneous, a laptop would have disturbed her intuition, she thought. For the others their connection to the internet had become part of their existence, they knew it and they appreciated to have the world's knowledge – and gossip – at their fingertips.

The event that had brought them together this time – it was not their first meeting – were last month's election results in several European countries. The extreme right, political parties with neo-fascist origins, had achieved landslide victories, a fundamental change of the political climate in Europe now could not be avoided any more. The next elections in England would be in two years – probably – but what now would happen on the continent certainly would heavily influence Britain's future.

Alpha and Omega were taking the role of the moderators of the discussion. Omega evidently was still influenced by his text – though the lines had stopped to talk to him a week ago. He was curious if the debate would be a substitution for the free-wheeling text. Alpha complemented Omega's dream walker lead by her practically oriented organisational talents. Or was it rather the other way round?

Omega took a zip from his coffee and put the cup back on the table. 'Can we still talk about just another episode of the East-West conflict, the continuing – now considerably hotter – Cold War?', he asked. Lucy was the first to respond, 'I don't think so. Neo-fascism in state power changes its physiognomy, its characteristic action set. That's what we saw in all historical experiences with fascism. Domestic fascist streamlining in all cultural aspects, a command economy to coordinate the supremacy of war industries, all that enforced by a police state. This is a new quality of social environment; and it now will happen in almost all European countries!'. Lucy's voice was calm, her excitement was carried by the content of her sentences. 'Yes.' Omega agreed, 'And the ideologically necessary aggressive nationalism together with the unavoidable domestic economic crises will force these regimes to go for military expansion, to lead wars in the name of their glorious nation. This is not just the historical lesson of the Nazi regime, it also occurred again and again in more recent wars.'. Alpha was looking at Omega, 'So, this is the end of the dream of a European unification process? I always have loved the image of a blooming of European creativity out of its diversity. Now, first the corporation-led institutional attempt of a European Union was exploded by incorporating Europe as part of the US military, and now the diverse set of disoriented European fascist regimes ruins the remainders of a common European goal.'. 'Probably there never had been a common European goal.', the silent Llewellin had to intervene. 'That's correct.', Barbarella felt she also should contribute something, 'I personally never had such a goal. All I wanted was to be free to travel wherever I wanted to go, to share secure and satisfying living circumstances with people in other countries.'. But Llewellin had aimed at something else with his remark, 'That's surely okay Barbarella, but I wanted to point out something different. Namely, that there never has been a proper agent to be called *Europe*. After the first re-construction years after the war there was only a group of European multinational corporations, the Copenhagen Round, which decided that they needed a political counterpart to transport their ambitions, the European Union. European social identity of the broad majority of the population till today is a side issue only. What is needed instead is the European consumer. To turn the globally produced commodities and services into money European consumers are pivotal, not only for European firms but in particular also for US firms. A consumer, a mass of individualized consumers, does not have a wish for a political identity bound to a geographical area, for being a European, a consumer only has a wish for a product – that's it. And without an agent, without this political entity Europeans being embedded in the brains of Europe's population, there is no *common European goal*.' 'That sounds frightening.', Lucy whispered. 'Why?', Alpha looked at her. Lucy explained, 'Because with a vacuum of political identity, this void in the brains of people is longing to be filled with something, with anything in principle. *Nature abhors a vacuum*, Aristotle knew already. And the only thing that fascists are good at is filling empty brains!'. Omega was stupefied, 'You always surprise me, Lucy. How can a young person like you be so educated? Aristotle!'. 'I am not educated, little regular schooling indeed. But I always have had my aunt Molly – and a stubborn curiosity.', she blushed a bit. 'Let's return to the interpretation of the recent election results.', she did not want to admit that the suspicion of Omega being flirting with Lucy had disturbed her, 'One probably also has to take into account that Western mass media in the last decade have been dominated in a breath-taking completeness by the agenda of the military, of boasting war propaganda. The unifying topic clearly was a war against Russia; and more recently against China and '*communism*' in general. In a predictable ideological countermove Russia has tried infiltrate local nationalist parties in Western Europe to support local nationalism as an opposition to US ideology. But while the anti-Russia front in military terms holds and even gets stronger, the ideological split-up has certain successes. This is what the elections show.'. Alpha looked around. 'When the Roman Empire was dissolving, it were the local vassals of Rome at the outskirts of the empire that turned out to be deadly menace for the central authority in Rome. They had been equipped with weapons and strategic military knowledge to enable expansion, so they were tempted to turn against their masters in the center.'. No, she was not trying to impress Omega with her knowledge. Alpha was just trying to come up with conclusions. 'I do not think that the time for the breakdown of the US empire has come.', Llewelyn doubted. 'Neither the conquest of Russia by NATO seems to be as close as certain circles in the US would like to have it. I rather predict a stalemate, without using a simulation model.', now Llewelyn smiled, 'You know, I had constructed one several years ago, built on some extensions of so-called General-Blotto Games.'. He stopped abruptly; no one knew about the things he talked about. Llewellyn had developed a fine sense to remark when he was going to be lonely. Then he should better direct his thoughts towards some inside dialog in his head – insane, he knew, but better to keep friendships alive. 'You mean that the exploitative empires of authoritarian capitalism in USA, Russia and China' - Alpha had discussed this characterisation with Omega – 'can coexist for a longer period alongside smaller wars at their respective borders?'. Llewelyn nodded. 'If you right, then we are further away from any kind of global communism than many of us thought.', Alpha sighed. 'Communism?', Barbarella had not been there when the text had talked to Omega about Marx' skepticism regarding social utopias. 'Can anybody give me a brief idea what we talk about when we mention communism?'. For a moment everybody was silent. 'You better call it *complete democracy* nowadays', Omega laughed a bit, but felt obliged to elaborate on his remark. 'The concept of democracy is a kind of self-reflective contradiction. Demos, the people, are thought to be their own rulers, the rulers are at the same time the ruled ones. On a linguistic level this is the archetype of an impossibility. You invent two opposites and at the same time state that they are the same. But now look what language is good for. In telling this impossibility, which linguistically cannot exist, to a class which is suffering from being ruled by an exploiting class, the wish to approach this impossibility in real life is amplified. The continuous battle in this process of approaching has a more innocent name. It's called progress.'. At that point Llewelyn, who often appreciated Barbarella's seemingly simple interventions – she was intellectually as archaic as he was – thought it was a good time to take over. 'It is the *delta* that is important.', Llewelyn said, 'You know in mathematics the Greek letter delta usually is used to denote the change of a variable per time unit.'. Now everybody understood – Llewelyn thought – for a few seconds. It was Lucy who came for help, 'The great German philosopher Frederic Engels expressed this in more vulgar words: *Bewegung ist die Daseinsform der Materie*, all matter is movement.'. 'You speak German?', now Alpha was astonished. 'No, I hardly speak a little Polish. But Molly speaks German, and she told me that the German version of this citation has a more aspiring aura. And I liked the way it sounds.'. Llewelyn wanted to continue, 'Okay, Engels wanted to connect the delta to the concept of matter. I am fine with that. But my point is even more subtle. In particular we humans are processing contradictions, as individuals as well as when we are tribes or classes. *Contradiction* in this context means that we *communicate* self-contradictory elements – within ourselves or within groups – to change our environment. We produce deltas of all the things that surround us. When we stop doing that, we are dead, and the environment produces some deltas with our dead corps. In other words, we are alive as long as we feel the contradiction in us that wants to be expressed. Just a variant on Lucy's claim for aura.'. Lucy thought for a moment that her associative impulse to mention Ornette Coleman would be in place, but Alpha was faster. 'Let me return to democracy.', she said, 'As class struggles proceed, in different continents and at different speed, it is the organizational setup of social institutions by which the approximation to democracy – or communism – is expressed. Thus, the delta in principle can be measured.'. It was not clear if this was a statement or a question. 'I think, it can at least be felt.'. This was Barbarella again. 'And I am sure', Barbarella could become serious too, 'that the undeniable feelings that each of us maintains, aggregates and accumulates will steer our languages and in the sequel our actions in a progressive direction, feelings will make delta big.'. They all stared at Barbarella. What was that? She had pinpointed that in class struggles it never should be forgotten that their ultimate compass was feeling, feeling shared by the concerned community. She had discovered communism all by herself. To take away a bit of the pathos in the room Barbarella quickly added her sentence: 'I am still waiting for the third sexual revolution.'. And she gave Llewelyn the eye.

19 SESSION LAMBDA

Two years later the radical global climate change had proceeded in a way that now reached the personal experiences of every individual on earth. Changes of the way of life were not only in the air, they suddenly were immediate necessities. The technical availability of communication devices had several severe consequences. It certainly amplified the multi- sided polarisation between different groups, since the stronger internal links did run parallel to stronger accentuated frontlines towards other groups. Increasing omnipresent polarisation was experienced as confusion, a clear self-explaining order of relevance was hard to see. In this atmosphere it was the time for self-promoting demagogues, offering their shallow 'explanations' of the world to globally powerful corporations and nationalist leaders maintaining their own warlords with their privately organised armies of mercenaries. For the average Joe, which US culture had produced in all Western infiltrated countries of the world, it was tempting, sometimes even unavoidable, to join one of the locally prevailing 'opinion-gangs'. Therefore, strong but completely unreliable convictions now were meeting deteriorating personal economic hardship.

It was late autumn when the cell met again in Henry's Hideaway. Alpha's insurance firm was doing well, the bankruptcies of some competitors in the market had increased the market share. It had never been so evident that the world was full of risk. But even for the biggest players it was clear that it would be a – financially - lethal event if one of the looming natural disasters would strike. The money on Omega's bank account was melting away much too fast. Interest rates had stayed low, too many extremely rich groups were looking for high-profit promising investment opportunities, while investment in these times was mainly state-driven investment in the weapons industry. The share of profit available for banks that came from productive investment of firms was shrinking, banks had to move closer to state administrations. Omega followed these developments closely; money markets always had interested him. To finance their weekly meetings still was no problem though for the two.

They had developed the habit to have a cup of coffee first, sometimes with a coke or a mineral water from the fridge. Then each of them said a few words on what had impressed her or him most in the last week. On that basis there immediately the content of their meeting crystallized. They had also introduced a rule that should keep the influence of the members somewhat in equilibrium: In a rotating order one of them should present an idea that had intrigued her or him. Today it was Llewellyn's turn. He liked this new rule.

'Do you all know Joseph-Louis Lagrange?', he started. 'We are not in school.', Barbarella thought, but did not say it. The question was rhetoric anyway. Llewellyn continued, 'Just to refresh your memories. Lagrange invented a most useful method of optimization, which in its more developed forms is used till today. He was a prodigy child brought up in Italy and at the age of 19 became professor of mathematics in Turin, later follower on the chair of Euler in Berlin. After his retirement he went to Paris, where he lived during the revolution. He became professor at the École Centrale des Travaux Publics, a university designed to train engineers in mathematics for the time after the revolution. But all that might only be interesting for those interested in topics on the interwovenness of the history of political economy and the history of mathematics. Like Lucy, perhaps.', Llewellyn had remarked some tiring faces, only Lucy seemed to be exceedingly attentive. Llewellyn had to change gear: 'Formal modelling can throw an interesting spotlight on the dynamics of a society. One of Lagrange's innovative solutions was directed on how to combine the search for an optimal value with side constraints that have to be met in the course of this search; to combine them in a single equation. Since his dissertation he had been fascinated by Leibniz invention of calculus, which he further developed extensively to treat the first part of his equation, the optimization of the goal variable. Th second part, the side constraints, could also be expressed as equations, usually as static equalities. Lagrange's path-breaking idea was to put these side constraints – collected between brackets – as an added term in the same goal optimizing equation, but multiplied with a new variable in front of the brackets. This new variable has become known as Lagrange's Lambda! With this technique Lagrange could solve his Lagrange function. The mysterious new variable, Lagrange's Lambda, had been introduces on abstract technical grounds only. But later on, applications of this technique in economics gave it a new interpretation. It was called the shadow price of the side constraints.'. Llewellyn looked around and saw the big 'Why' in the eyes of his friends. What had all this to do with their task to interpret important events in contemporary political economy?

Llewellyn saw that he had to continue, 'Now think of all the quickly worsening environmental conditions that surround us as side constraints – the second part of the Lagrange function. What is the first part, which relentlessly is maximized and drives our society? It clearly is what has been called the capitalist algorithm, making the highest short-term profit with the lowest risk – on all levels of social institutions, down to the individuals that subscribe to reduce themselves to ego-firms.'. Now the others understood. 'What about the magical number, Lagrange's Lambda? I guess it is the shadow price of environmental destruction?', this was Alpha with her rapid and practice-oriented mind. 'Exactly. It is a shadow of factors because we, the population, only feels it. It does not directly enter the optimization calculus of those who run capitalism. Only via some measures enforced by state power our 'feelings' become side constraints for the central decision-makers. And in the last year Lagrange's Lambda did increase tremendously, I have to say.'.
Llewellyn seemed to be content, the others were perplexed. He had to add a caveat: 'This, of course, is a very rigid and abstract interpretation of what is going on. It misses all colourful detail and does not pay attention to the further formal developments since Lagrange's first formulation. But I think it is an interesting starting point for our discussion.'. This was correct, later they all would remember this meeting as the *Lambda Session.*

During the last months Barbarella and Lucy had been participating in efforts pushing for more environmental protection, mainly via state regulations. 'You mean that the increasing Lambda coefficient is the felt, but economically invisible force that works via the influence on the state to tighten environmental controls, if I understood you correctly?', Barbarella asked. 'And this transforms our problem with the environmental constrains into a problem of the split-up of government expenditure. If most of this expenditure goes into war equipment, then little is left our 'side constraint'. Moreover, the big environmental problems can only be dealt with on a global level, whereas spending money on the own nationalist army becomes a zero-sum game – with actual local wars but also with stalemates of mutual deterrence.', Lucy was taking the interpretation to the next topic, the role of the state. Omega chimed in, 'It is a multi- facetted dilemma. The ruling state is the state of the ruling class, sometimes with some inlets for lower social strata if the majority of exploitation runs via exchange rates of the poor South. The rulers in the nation state will fail to keep Lambda low because their actions remain local, they thus will turn to diversion, to pointless nationalist rhetoric. Lagrange's Lambda becomes the victim of a prisoners' dilemma game between nationalist countries.'. He looked at Llewellyn.

Alpha chipped in, 'Maybe it needs a more radical step. What if the side-constraint becomes a goal function and the former goal is reduced to a side-constraint? Of course, this implies somewhat different interpretations of what the two are. What are the goal levels of the variables in the former side-constraints? And what is the fixed minimum rate of accumulation of physical goods that has to be met as the new side constraint. What formally looks like a simple dual problem indeed implies qualitative jumps in interpretation. This also concerns the new Lagrange's Lambda, or am I wrong?'. Llewellyn did not know if Alpha asked him, he was surprised and a bit confused by the ideas that his presentation had stimulated. Interpretation was not his strong side, rather the opposite: Escaping into abstract spaces. The shadow price of the necessary physical accumulation was not an easy topic. It certainly had to be determined by simultaneously solving the whole system, the entire Lagrange function. All optimally envisaged levels of environmental variables played a role.

And then Llewellyn's thoughts suddenly jumped to his days as a young student, second semester. This was the time when his initiation as a member of the invisible group of critical, left-leaning students happened. What he remembered was a standard question that they regularly asked professors of mathematical economics. The question was: 'Whose function is that?'. In his later studies of theoretical physics, the question did not make much sense; functions seemed to be just innocent presentations of laws of physics. Maybe they were a bit distorted by the belief of the interpreter, like Kepler's law for the masses of planets, and could be improved as religious or quasi-religious prejudices were eliminated. But compared to the functions concerning the human society, these functions had the air of being neutral. The interpretation of the Lagrange function they were just discussing was definitely not neutral, Llewellyn thought. So: 'Whose function was that?'.

The original version had revealed several agents: The omnipresent capitalist algorithm, the global biosystem including the majority of the world's population, the state, classes in the rich North and classes in the poor South. Alpha's new, inverted interpretation of the Lagrange function mainly pointed at one most important new agent: A global government that could determine the optimal environmental levels and thus would be able to limit physical accumulation to the necessary level. Lagrange's Lambda of the new system in this case would have left the sphere of feelings. It would have become an ultimate global policy index, which would align growth decisions that could be taken by global economic policy. Of course, the political agent that could take these decisions, a democratically legalised world government had to be put in place first. Didn't that point back to the so-called Delta session, which Llewellyn faintly remembered? Llewellyn had not spoken a word so far; now the looks of the four other members showed that they expected Llewellyn to answer Alpha's question.

Llewellyn did not want to bother them with stories about his student days, the circumventing arguments in his introductory statement had been tedious enough for them. He took the easy way out, 'Yes, you are right, Alpha.'. It sounded shy. Too shy, he felt and added a kind of upshot of his internal thought process, 'This number, Lagrange's Lambda of the new system, has to serve as the limit for something called *overall physical growth*. How to compute it is a problem of its own, since the necessary replacement investment – it's sectoral growth rate - in different sectors of the global production system will vary and will be highly interdependent. Moreover, to enable the aggregation of different physical growth rates given in physical units, a monetary system, a new kind of monetary system will be necessary. The old kind of monetary system had been tailored to serve the old kind optimization goal, which was maximum exploitation. The new monetary system will have to have something in common with the old system, namely that it avoids, indeed transcends, the measurement units of the physical quantities monitored, it will have to be metaphysical. My guess is that it will involve time measurement. Let's leave it like that. And I briefly have thought about a question implicit in Alpha's radical inversion of the old abstract system. Which forces in real economic and political life are able to enforce it?', Llewellyn hesitated; he already had talked too long for what he had planned as a brief upshot.

It was one of these moments when Omega admired Llewellyn. Contrary to his own experience of being the slave of his text, Llewellyn always was the master of his sentences, he controlled them. This was most visible in moments when he consciously stopped an episode. His text had never learned to stop its flow, it always called for his fingertips. Even now, after a long time of abstinence, he heard his text very softly calling. The only calls for his fingertips, for his body, that always were stronger than those of his text were the calls of Alpha. They drowned his text. Thinking about Alpha instantly made Omega happy. His life was perfect, wasn't it? Alpha, their meetings in Henry's Hideaway, eventually his duties as mouthpiece of his text again. Despite the impasse that authoritarian global capitalism was heading to, despite worsening living conditions, despite the never-ending danger of a war nearby, despite all that Omega felt strong and happy. 'You smile?', Lucy asked Omega who had been falling in a daydream and had not followed the ongoing discussion in the session. 'Optimism is an indispensable ingredient of each progressive action.', they both knew that it was just a one-size-fits-it-all sentence was, meant to hide his absence. 'We were just talking about Lagrange and the possibility that the evolution of abstract concepts leads a life of its own. Many theoretical attempts lead nowhere, but a few of them turn out as theoretical breakthroughs. My argument was that the direction of theoretical evolution does only partly emerge out of the wish to overcome an existing theoretical problem. More often it is stimulated by problems in the world outside the theory – least in the long-run.'. 'Oh, you were talking about innovation.', Omega was heading for the next daydream.

20 TANGO WAVES

Barbarella was a curvy woman, Lucy not so much. Alpha was in between. The shapes of the two men were average, not too fat, no beards. 'Well, good times follow bad times, followed by good times and so on. And there is always something new.', she said and felt a bit stupid. 'Women looking at men seem to have a simpler categorization than the other way round: Either acceptable, or unacceptable. The truth probably was that they are less interested in men than men in women.', Barbarella thought - and that she was an outlier. She loved to be curvy, only curves in your head allow you to gain different perspectives on what your senses let enter.

Llewellyn always had been fascinated by calculus. He sometimes wished to have lived in the times of Newton and Leibniz, a time when understanding the congruence of mathematics and physics enabled them to invent a blissful new method, which provided a giant step of understanding in both fields. What was attacked by these two transdisciplinary heroes of science was the non-linearity of the world: Gravity clearly was non-linear with respect to distance as most diagrams depicting suspicious relationships of empirically observed variables were not linear. How shrinking time or distance could lead to the well-defined new formalism of derivatives, which then by the inverting the procedure allowed for integrals – the non- symmetric detection of what had produced the derivatives in the first place. Non-linearity allowed – but did not force – to return to the origin of a movement in time and space, spirals and waves were its simplest appearances. This was Llewellyn's world; this was where he felt at home. After Barbarella's clumsy sentence he didn't want to show off with his more elaborated view on 'waves'. All he contributed was: 'Yeah – the non-linearity of waves. With each wave a new direction can – but need not – be discovered. That is the main thrust of waves with respect to progress. With this additional feature waves become spiral.'

Alpha was the one who had initiated the they all thought for some moment on waves, while sitting there with their coffee cups just before the meeting started.

She wanted to share a very personal feeling about her life. As the pseudo-boss of Barbarella and Lucy there still remained a little distance, despite the fact that they now were very close. Llewellyn had been Omega's friend first and usually did not want to be too closely involved in the private life of others. And Omega did not count since he knew almost everything about her. 'I am going through a kind of long-run waves in my life.', she said, 'In the first stage I was just thrown in a pre-defined setting. Not much of a choice, though at that time I did not recognize this. Then I was trying to establish myself by living with a partner, with limited success.', she thought about Frank, 'Finally – and to my great surprise – I met the love of my life: Omega. With him my development as an individual personality seemed to be complete. And in so far as my person is concerned, this still is correct.'. The short break she made now, let everybody become curious. They all knew that the two were a couple. She continued, 'But I am a part of society and with a political landscape that moves towards right-wing autocratic regimes I realized that I have to be – and, yes, I want to be – a *political animal*. This part of my personality started to run parallel to my love life with Omega. It worked, but the additional link between Omega and me that was necessary also had its price. We had to work on this new type of unity that we now were experiencing. In the last year we reached that productive harmony again – including the creative contradictions, the dis-equilibrium episodes – that gave a thrill to our cooperation.', a short break again, 'So, my life is running through *long-run waves*: getting close to something, loosing something somewhat, finding new directions and new energy, experience some boredom, and so on.'. Alpha had to stop, her emotions had been swelling and the reference to waves had been a tool to move her thoughts towards more neutral grounds.

Omega was moved too, and he had recognized Alpha's attempt to escape from too personal confessions. 'So true Alpha! Our lives can be understood as sequences of waves with only one predetermined direction, namely aging. Notwithstanding this personal experience, the falling apart into human individuals for the greater part is an illusion. We are all bound in a tightly knit web of interdependencies.', now they both were on the save grounds of a theoretical discussion. 'Societies also in many respects are moving along long-run cycles, economists call them Kondratieff cycles or stages of social accumulation.' This was the point of time when Barbarella and Llewellyn had started their contributions concerning curves and non-linearity.

After Llewellyn's words everybody had finished the coffee. It was Lucy's turn in this meeting to propose a topic. Of course, the talk about waves had left a trace in her mind too. 'What we are currently seeing in the world economy is that things are not turning as bad as we have feared five years ago, when we started our meetings. Global exploitation has become pretty stable, the most dystopian scenarios have turned out to be wrong, or at least pre-mature. For me, I am the youngest one in our cell, this is not necessarily bad news, though. This might be the lower turning point of a long-run wave in socio-economic life of the global economy. I might expect to be entering a long-run up-swing in my coming adult life. As a consequence, we should ask ourselves if we need this cell anymore. Or, if we should at least change some of its basic, unwritten assumptions. Where are the cracks in authoritarian global capitalism today? Are they widening? Have new cracks appeared? Or, – to ask a provocative question – is this type of capitalism rather long-lasting, say another 500 years?'.

'That is interesting. You are right, Lucy, one tends to predict that fundamental improvements, social revolutions will happen during one's lifetime. And, as different generations have different life expectations, the one with the shortest life expectation has already been somewhat frustrated if the development during their lifetime had mostly been not progressive enough.', Omega was not knowing what he wanted to say, 'And the cracks … we rarely get information on what is happening in the top spheres of decision-makers in industry and military. Mass media only distribute information in a strategic way. Most of it is meant for tranquilizing and stream-lining the public opinion. There are some long-run waves in these mass media politics, mainly produced by local border conflicts, which occasionally turn into minor wars. But most tectonic shifts in global political economy dynamics remain in the dark.'

Llewellyn had to add something, 'I think it is important to distinguish between visible waves in the mass media and less visible processes, vibrations, in the background. Considered in a more general way, the starting points are the sources of these vibrations. There are more than 8 billion human individuals, most of them in definite locations; then there are the social organisations and institutions they are forming. Each one also emitting waves of different amplitude and frequency. They range from family, tribe, class and language community to more explicitly economic and political entities. It is not only a mass of heterogenous entities, it is a mess. All waves emitted by them are overlapping, though usually a smaller entity's power to radiate is restricted by the power of the larger entity in which it is embedded. Mass media are just the technological tool that enables a move towards this social master-slave principle. But perhaps we should drop the approach to start with relevant entities. We could also start by assuming that our object of investigation is a set of *overlaying fields*, like theoretical physics nowadays starts. We then would characterize a social institution only by frequency and mass, by its momentum – where it exists, where it materializes as a physical entity, is only described as a probability. This is similar to describing the position of an electron with the help of the Schrödinger equation. To be even more speculative: the links between entities might then be the entanglement of more or less neighbouring different momenta.'. Now Llewellyn definitely was alone in the room – a nerd.

Alpha came to rescue, 'How can we interpret *frequency* and *mass* as elements of social dynamics? How about viewing frequency as a measure of strength with which a certain *contradiction* pushes to be solved; a bit like electrical voltage? While mass in your speculation could be understood as *power*, the power with which a certain frequency is able to override and modulate neighbouring momenta. This power, exerted on the surrounding space then defines a metric of that space isn't it Llewellyn?'. She had to play a bit the nerd too. Llewellyn nodded, he understood.

Now it was Barbarella's time to tear the arguments down to solid ground again, 'Thank you, Alpha. It's much easier for me to think in terms of contradictions and power. I often feel terribly unfit to what happens around me, I feel this contradiction. And it results in my wavy behaviour, though my power is too weak to change much in my environment.'. Alpha liked Barbarella a lot, she continued in the same vein, 'I remember to have watched this famous old movie with Marylin Monroe, I think it was called 'Misfits'. It was a film about characters that were contradictory to the society that was emerging around them. It parallels another French movie of the time - À bout de souffle from 1960 - in a sense these movies were forerunners of 'Easy Rider' the hymn on drop-outs. They all were based on the idea of individual contradictions. The social power of these films consisted in the fact that seeing a personally experienced contradiction displayed – and eventually dissolved – in a movie character strengthens its force, gives it more power. It is not surprising that twenty years later, in the Reagan era, Hollywood adapted its tremendous power to the needs of the conservative government. Today all movies produced there have first to be seen and approved by the ministry of war, which officially has the misleading name Department of Defense.'.

Lucy had watched Barbarella while listening to Alpha. Barbarella evidently felt justified by Alpha's trip into the world of movies, though she mumbled that she had seen none of these films. She only had heard of 'Easy Rider' being a cult movie for boomers. Now Barbarella went to the fridge and got herself a beer. Lucy knew that the concept of a 'contradiction' had resulted in heavy debates in Marxist circles since Lenin's time. More recently a famous conflict was which contradiction should be considered as the dominant contradiction, the contradiction between exploited and exploiters or the contradiction between women and men. In her view this dispute had nothing to do with Marx, in the 19th century 'Marxism' simply didn't exist, these progressive theories only just were born, and the same is true for feminism. With the frequency interpretation of contradictions, it was easy to argue that the two contradictions in question were simply overlapping frequencies of unfit state of affairs in today's society. She did not know why, but out of her thoughts Lucy suddenly said rather loud – and without an apparent connection to what has just been talked about: 'It takes two to Tango!'

Everybody was puzzled. 'What ?!', Omega had used this saying several times in recent times. 'I just was in my thoughts, sorry. Probably I wanted to express that a contradiction, a thrill, a wave needs two poles to swing.', Lucy excused her unfit remark. 'At least two attractors,' Omega had become interested. 'And it produces a third element, namely a change of direction. It rather is a spiral.', he said with a glance to Llewellyn. 'You are not really talking about dancing the Tango, I hope.', Barbarella protested. 'I hate Tango, I hate all these dances with predefined step sequences. Who is it, 'The Tango'? Is it a subject that is allowed to determine that only two individuals may dance it? Why not three?'. Several voices now were interfering in a cacophonic intermezzo.

Llewellyn: 'With three with interaction between them you run into the dangers of the 3-body problem, even a deterministically-minded dancing school would be despaired, since slightly different starting positions would usually drive dancers into hundreds of very different shapes of movements. Tango would explode into hundreds of completely different Tangos.'

Omega: 'Tango is not a subject, correct. But it is an elementary guidance, a framework within which additional creative moves can find their place. A framework gives you security, in particular as a beginner. In Hegelian terms, the emergence of a synthesis between Tango rules and creative expansion of these rules can be experimented with. And those dancers that watch a pair of masters in this art will be inspired to follow them. It is a good thing to have a frame - and to play to perforate it.'

Alpha: 'Okay, forget the Tango spirals. Just think about understanding what happened in the past; your own past or the past of mankind, does not matter. To get an idea what might happen in the future – the major reason for storing memories - you need to periodize what happened in the past. You have to find patterns, to identify waves. 'Waves', I think, is something you can accept – down there at earth. 'Tango' you can replace by any other illusion that fires your imagination.'

Barbarella was not good in multi-tasking of that kind. The three parallel statements of her friends for her were like an extremely noisy motor bike passing by. She shook her head, not unfriendly, but signaling that she did not plan to insist on what she had said. After a moment of exhaustion, it was Lucy again who restarted the Tango wave topic. She was much better in multi-tasking.

'I have to confess that I only was captured by the catchy saying, this 'it takes two to Tango'. I don't know much about Tango and frankly, like you Barbarella, I find ballroom dancing awful. When I think of Argentinian Tango, I think on Argentina first – and since December 2023 Argentina is a tragic case. Latin American dances often reflect a mixture between patriarchal dominance, catholic anxiousness with respect to sex, and an exaggerated romantic beauty with respect to music. Having said that, having expressed a certain aversion, I have to admit that combining an illustrative concept like 'wave' - ranging from nature to mathematics – with the flair of strange beauty, which is also in the associative circle surrounding 'Tango', attracts me. I think this sensual attraction is what has been called aesthetic, a feeling that emerges before perception has been sent through the machinery of rationalisation. I personally know aesthetics mainly from my encounters with the domain of music.'. Barbarella was nodding vehemently, though she thought about a different kind of music than Lucy. 'This is a peculiar type of domain. There, the very personal experience of presence meets the presence of something outside yourself; so fast that it cannot be understood in the rational way of understanding after an explanation. In that experience I am - you are - completely alone. Like the great drug addict Miles Davies when he plays his solo – he still is alive. What I wanted to contribute to our cell in this meeting is simply that I have a similar, purely intuitive feeling that society is going to pass through its lower turning point in the next decade. This intuition does not result in a contemplative waiting position. At least for me, generation Z as you have called me once, it is a call to action. We are not approaching the end of time but – as the Nobel prize winner Roger Penrose could have said – we are walking in spirals.'. 'Penrose?!', Llewellyn and Alpha exclaimed unisono. 'Sorry, I only wanted to avoid to use the infamous expression Tango waves again.', Lucy smiled.

EPILOGUE

A couple of years had gone by when the text appeared again. It appeared in Omega's head; he had no laptop at hand. It was softly whispering, 'You know, Omega, all fairy tales start with 'Once upon a time …'. Now, I am not a fairy tale. I am about the future, the near future. And since it has arrived now, I have to vanish …'.

The sessions of the cell in Henry's Hideaway had ended. Only Barbarella was still living in London trying to initiate the third sexual revolution. Llewellyn had been offered a professorship in Barcelona, which he gladly accepted. There he found colleagues, which over

the time replaced his close relationship to Omega. Alpha and Omega had visited him there during Alpha's holydays and spent a formidable month in the sun. For their retirement they plan to live on one of the southern islands of Spain or Portugal. They still are in love with each other. Lucy moved to Scotland. After her aunt Molly had died, she followed her new friend Desmond to Glasgow, who had found a lucrative occupation in a design firm there. And Lucy started to sing in a band in the evening to earn some additional money – and have some fun.

MYSTERIOUS LINKS

Chapter 1

Social Identity and Class Consciousness (2018):

https://www.tandfonline.com/doi/full/10.1080/07360932.2018.1447495

Chapter 2

Bridges to Babylon (2014):

http://www.econ.tuwien.ac.at/hanappi/Papers/Hanappi_2014j_Babylon_opt.pdf

Chapter 3

Honey Pie: https://www.youtube.com/watch?v=0Sr0efOe8yk

Girl: https://www.youtube.com/watch?v=-8l3ntDR_ll

Chapter 4

All You Need Is Love: https://www.youtube.com/watch?v=4EGczv7iiEk

Can Europe Survive? Ten Commandments for Europe's Next Ten Years (2013):

http://www.econ.tuwien.ac.at/hanappi/Papers/Hanappi_2013i.pdf

From Growth to Innovative Reproduction (2010):

http://mpra.ub.uni-muenchen.de/29062/

Cry for Love:

https://www.youtube.com/watch?v=rmEZlbTp8N8

Chapter 5

Cross Town Traffic: https://www.youtube.com/watch?v=nqb3R2fijpQ

Nowhere Man: https://www.youtube.com/watch?v=8scSwaKbE64

I Can't Give You Anything but Love: https://www.youtube.com/watch?v=fc_60l9u7fg

Chapter 6

Learning by Trying (1997):
http://www.econ.tuwien.ac.at/hanappi/Papers/Hanappi-Egger_Hanappi_1997.pdf

The Fool on the Hill: https://www.youtube.com/watch?v=wsRatIMUSu8

Sign Systems of Lust and Slavery (2023):

https://link.springer.com/article/10.1007/s43253-023-00103-z

Chapter 7

Alarm. The evolutionary jump of global political economy needed (2020):

http://www.paecon.net/PAEReview/issue94/Hanappi94.pdf

Collect now - Consume later (2003):

http://www.econ.tuwien.ac.at/hanappi/Papers/hanappi_2003c.pdf

Paperback Writer: https://www.youtube.com/watch?v=rjZCViOokEY

Chapter 8

Besame Mucho: https://www.youtube.com/watch?v=y0VwQXnkDqU

Ramona: https://www.youtube.com/watch?v=BBlMF0aLoV4

Chapter 9

Agent-based modelling. History-Essence-Future (2007):

https://legacy.econ.tuwien.ac.at/hanappi/Papers/Hanappi_2017z_14154-26924-1-PB.pdf

Russia. The Background of the Russian Invasion of Ukraine (2022):

https://journals.aserspublishing.eu/tpref/article/view/7466

Back in the USSR: https://www.youtube.com/watch?v=hhanYixwfSU

Norbert Wiener's Cybernetic Critique of the Information Society (1998):

http://www.econ.tuwien.ac.at/hanappi/Papers/Hanappi_Hanappi-Egger_2001.pdf

Chapter 10

Signs of Reality - Reality of Signs (2011): http://mpra.ub.uni-muenchen.de/31570/

The Times They are Changing:

https://www.youtube.com/watch?v=90WD_ats6eE&list=RD90WD_ats6eE&start_radio=1

Let it ride: https://www.youtube.com/watch?v=as9rkVyMpNA

Chapter 11

Perplexing Complexity. Human Modelling and Primacy of the Group as Essence of Complexity (2020):

https://legacy.econ.tuwien.ac.at/hanappi/Papers/Hanappi_2020e.pdf

Humanism or Racism (2018):

https://mpra.ub.uni-muenchen.de/87658/

San Francisco Nights: https://www.youtube.com/watch?v=_FKRIK5jQzs

Everybody's Got Something To Hide Except Me And My Monkey:

https://www.youtube.com/watch?v=eyV3zCq1OHM

Maxwell's Demons in Brains and Politics (2003):

http://www.econ.tuwien.ac.at/hanappi/Papers/Maxwell.pdf

Chapter 12

Hey Bulldog: https://www.youtube.com/watch?v=M4vbJQ-MrKo

Yellow Submarine:

https://www.youtube.com/watch?v=m2uTFF_3MaA

Diversity of Diversity (2013):

http://www.econ.tuwien.ac.at/hanappi/Papers/Hanappi_Hanappi-Egger_2013b_(New_York).pdf

The Neumann-Morgenstern Project (2013):

http://www.econ.tuwien.ac.at/hanappi/Papers/Hanappi_2013g_Chpt1.pdf

Metamorphosis in Political Economy. A new combination of three disparate ideas (2017):

https://legacy.econ.tuwien.ac.at/hanappi/Papers/Hanappi_2018a-Three_Ideas.pdf

Chapter 13

Information Age - Deformation Age - Reformation Age (1994):

http://www.econ.tuwien.ac.at/hanappi/Papers/Hanappi_Egger_1993b.pdf

Hold Tight: https://www.youtube.com/watch?v=1iHG7YRorgM

Satisfaction: https://www.youtube.com/watch?v=NEjkftp7J7I

Chapter 14

On the Eve of Global Financial Collapse (2008):

http://www.econ.tuwien.ac.at/hanappi/Papers/EAEPE2008.pdf

Capital after Capitalism (2018):

https://www.jstor.org/stable/10.13169/worlrevipoliecon.9.1.0061?seq=1#page_scan_tab_contents

Good Vibrations: https://www.youtube.com/watch?v=Eab_beh07HU

Chapter 15

Evolutionary Political Economy in Crisis Mode (2014):

http://www.jbnst.de/de/inhalte.php?id=23402

NATO Expansion versus Consolidation of the EU (2017):

http://www.econ.tuwien.ac.at/hanappi/Papers/Hanappi_2016n_(NATO-EU).pdf

Lucy In the Sky with Diamonds: https://www.youtube.com/watch?v=naoknj1ebqI

Chapter 16

The Dynamics of the Global Political Economy (2007):

https://legacy.econ.tuwien.ac.at/hanappi/Papers/Cuba_2007.pdf

From Integrated Capitalism to Disintegrating Capitalism. Scenarios of a Third World War (2019):

https://arpejournal.com/article/id/163/

New Combinations. Taking Schumpeter's concept serious (2007):

http://mpra.ub.uni-muenchen.de/28396/

Chapter 17

The Concept of Choice - Why and how innovative behaviour is not just stochastic (2005):

http://www.econ.tuwien.ac.at/hanappi/Papers/Hanappi_2008.pdf

Money, Credit, Capital, and the State (2013):

http://www.econ.tuwien.ac.at/hanappi/Papers/Hanappi_2013c.pdf

Bitches Brew:

https://www.youtube.com/watch?v=o2H7MHA5Qqw

Endogenous Needs, Values and Technology (2006):

https://mpra.ub.uni-muenchen.de/28880/1/MPRA_paper_28880.pdf

The Survival of the Fattest (2004): http://mpra.ub.uni-muenchen.de/29424/

Chapter 18

The Beat of Visions (2010): https://mpra.ub.uni-muenchen.de/28398/

From Growth to Innovative Reproduction. A Roadmap for a European Model of Evolution (2010):

https://mpra.ub.uni-muenchen.de/29062/1/MPRA_paper_29062.pdf

Free Jazz: https://www.youtube.com/watch?v=8bRTFr0ytA8

Chapter 19

Elements of an I-O-based Framework for Marxian, Feminist and World-System Approaches (2003):

https://legacy.econ.tuwien.ac.at/hanappi/Papers/Hanappi_2003a.pdf

Evolutionary Economic Programs (2004):

https://legacy.econ.tuwien.ac.at/hanappi/Papers/Hanappi_2004e.pdf

Evolutionary Political Economy: Content and Methods. (2015):

https://www.tandfonline.com/doi/full/10.1080/07360932.2017.1287748

Classes - From National to Global Class Formation (2018):

https://www.intechopen.com/chapters/63535

Chapter 20

Imagine: https://www.youtube.com/watch?v=EcPsB6PwaiE

Shangri-La Governance (2012):

https://legacy.econ.tuwien.ac.at/hanappi/Papers/Hanappi_2012s.pdf

Defeating Nationalism in Europe (2015):

https://legacy.econ.tuwien.ac.at/hanappi/Papers/Hanappi_2015a.pdf

Embedded in Global Politics (2014):

https://legacy.econ.tuwien.ac.at/hanappi/Papers/Hanappi_2014e.pdf

Complex World Money (2024):

https://mpra.ub.uni-muenchen.de/106285/1/MPRA_paper_106285.pdf

Atlantis Rising. Blueprint for a Better World (2022):

https://legacy.econ.tuwien.ac.at/hanappi/Papers/Hanappi_2022e_JAES_Atlantis_Rising.pdf

Europa: https://www.youtube.com/watch?v=h4Mrp6wuSwk

Epilogue

The Death of the Family? (2005):

https://legacy.econ.tuwien.ac.at/hanappi/Papers/EAEPE2005.pdf

Ob-La-Di, Ob-La-Da: https://www.youtube.com/watch?v=_J9NpHKrKMw

Predictions and Hopes. Global Political Economy Dynamics of the next Ten Years (2024):

https://journals.scholarpublishing.org/index.php/ASSRJ/article/view/17381

ABOUT THE AUTHOR

Hardy Hanappi was born in Vienna and studied economics and Informatics. He became university professor and researcher at the University of Technology of Vienna and concentrated on macroeconomics, political economy, simulation methods, and game theory. He was deputy director of socioeconomics at the Austrian Academy of Sciences, and director of the Institute for Monetary Economics (Ludwig Boltzmann-Institute). From 2004 till 2016 he was Scientific Development Officer of the European Association for Evolutionary Political Economy. From 2011 to 2015 he was professorial research associate at SOAS (University of London). He currently is ad personam chair for Political Economy at the European Commission and director of the Vienna Institute for Political Economy Research (VIPER). For more details on his curriculum vitae see http://www.econ.tuwien.ac.at/hanappi/cv_Hanappi.pdf .

He has been project leader of numerous research projects and author of more than 200 publications:
http://www.econ.tuwien.ac.at/hanappi/publications.html

He is married to professor Edeltraud Hanappi-Egger, has three children and lives in Vienna.

Printed in Poland
by Amazon Fulfillment
Poland Sp. z o.o., Wrocław
04 November 2024

354acd5f-76e1-46ce-bef8-ceaf7d169357R01